the ties that bind

the ties that bind

Six journeys of a lifetime

Julietta Jameson

BANTAM BOOKS
SYDNEY • AUCKLAND • TORONTO • NEW YORK • LONDON

THE TIES THAT BIND
BANTAM BOOK

First published in Australia and New Zealand in 2002
by Bantam

National Library of Australia
Cataloguing-in-Publication Entry

Jameson, Julietta, 1963–.
The ties that bind: six journeys of a lifetime.

ISBN 1 86325 381 5.

1. Family reunions. 2. Immigrants – Australia – Family
relationships. 3. Children of immigrants – Australia –
Family relationships. 4. Australia – Emigration and
immigration – Social aspects. 5. Australia – Genealogy. I.
Title.

306.85

Transworld Publishers,
a division of Random House Australia Pty Ltd
20 Alfred Street, Milsons Point, NSW 2061
http://www.randomhouse.com.au

Random House New Zealand Limited
18 Poland Road, Glenfield, Auckland

Transworld Publishers,
a division of The Random House Group Ltd
61–63 Uxbridge Road, London W5 5SA

Random House Inc
1540 Broadway, New York, New York 10036

Cover design by Ignition Brands
Photography by Joanna Kelly and David Kelly
Internal design by Tina Jantke
Typeset in 12/16 pt Sabon by Midland Typesetters, Maryborough, Victoria
Printed and bound by Griffin Press, Netley, South Australia

10 9 8 7 6 5 4 3 2 1

Contents

Foreword
Eden Gaha and Dave Kelly

What motivates someone to take on a particular task when everyone around them is saying 'Don't!'?

Over the last two and a half years of producing *The Ties That Bind* this is a question that we've had to ask ourselves time and time again.

We'd like to say that the answer is 'Passion!' An unquestioning desire to make something 'worthwhile', to 'speak to people', to 'touch their hearts' and (here's a beauty) 'to make a difference'.

Of course, that's all bullshit. The real motivating factor in most of these situations, certainly ours, is stubbornness. You see, we're the kind of people who want to prove the impossible, particularly if we're constantly told that it can't be done. Which is why we must now offer our sincerest thanks to those many funding bodies, television executives, sponsors and celebrities who said 'No'. In all honesty, it was their defiance coupled with our own that finally brought *The Ties That Bind* to the screen.

Eden: It all started for me in early 1999. I was out of work in Melbourne living off my wife, Nicola, who was performing in the musical, *Chicago*. With no prospects until later in the year, I would spend my days pacing our flat, watching TV, hitting the gym and basically wondering what the hell I was going to do with my life. I decided to do something related to television and thought, why not write something? Great, but what? For a while I dicked around with a film script, treatments and format ideas, none of which really drove me.

Finally it came to me. I thought back to my school-yard days when I was an ethnic-looking boy with an Anglo–Australian upbringing. I was one of those kids who fell between the gaps, drifting around the playground between the wogs who looked like me and the Aussies who acted like me – none of whom I fully understood. Basically I had an identity crisis. As the son of a Lebanese father and an Irish Catholic mother, both born in Australia, I had a foot in both cultural camps. Well, actually, that's a lie. I was very Australian and didn't really understand a thing about my Lebanese heritage, except the food, which I loved.

Approaching thirty, I knew that there were some questions about my identity that had to be answered. And not just by asking relatives, but by finding the answers myself, first hand. I had always had a burning desire to see Lebanon, something that hadn't been possible while civil war was raging.

To be honest, at the forefront of my mind was the question: How can I get to Lebanon and get someone else to pay for it? Then the idea of making a documentary of my first journey to the homeland emerged. Of course, it was extremely pig-headed of me to assume that my own story would be gripping enough and worthy of documenting on film, a point that, luckily, didn't escape me at the time.

I knew my own story would be less than interesting at

best. But what I also knew was that the story of my then ninety-three-year-old grandfather, Naseeb, was infinitely more interesting and that a journey about a young man making his first trip to Lebanon with his grandfather making his last was potentially worth putting a camera in front of.

This was the seed of *The Ties That Bind*, a name that was attached to my new, all-consuming passion as a 'working title', a name that a few TV programmers suggested would eventually need to be changed as it was 'too soft'. And yet, a name that could never be topped as a way of most simply explaining the idea. For me, *The Ties That Bind* was a name that perfectly encapsulated the way I felt, as well as what I believed was the situation among ethnic Australians in this day and age.

Let me explain. Since immigration was first embraced in the fifties and sixties out of a need for skilled and unskilled labour in this country, Australia's national identity has been set on a course for change. From then on it was always only going to be a matter of time before the bronzed, blond, chesty-bond image of Australia was going to be completely transformed. I genuinely believe that Australia's identity – that face of Australia, what we look like as a nation – is yet to be formed. In fact, if we are honest with ourselves, in years to come, the typical Australian, the dinky-dye, will probably look Eurasian. Interesting thought.

Australia is perhaps the most successful multicultural model ever. Look at the Thai, Lebanese, Italian and Chinese restaurants you can eat at just down the road from where you live. How many Greek cafés have you been to this year or Vietnamese bakeries? Look at the amount of religions that are freely practised without fear of persecution. We are truly a society that has been enriched by the many cultures we have welcomed to our shores.

Australia is also an interesting place in that the cultures from which our ancestors have come have been encouraged to flourish since their arrival. Australians are not expected to stand under a new flag and denounce all that they have left behind in their countries of origin. Rather, we have developed microcosms of the lands left behind, all melding together to form one of the most interesting and largely tolerant societies on the planet.

So this brings me back to *The Ties That Bind*, because I believe that these are the cultural ties that our parents and grandparents have hung on to and taught us throughout our childhood. For example, young Greek kids spend a few hours each day after school attending Greek school. They understand much of what it means to be Greek whilst perhaps never having visited Greece. They are Greek–Australians, they have a foot in both camps.

Sometimes for them, as with myself, there is a void, a series of questions that can only be answered with a visit back to the birthplace of their ancestors. We've heard the stories, seen the photos, but like with most things, nothing will quite resonate until we have experienced it first hand. At least that was the driving factor for me and, as I later discovered, a feeling shared by many young first and second generation Australians.

As a young boy, I would sit at my grandparents' place after school every Monday and listen to stories of an old country I had never seen, of aunts, uncles and cousins I had never met, of 'Lebanon, the Paris of the Middle East'. The same country that I would watch on the six o'clock news, being devastated by civil war and foreign invasion. This was my mixed impression.

So the desire to go and find out a little bit more about how I ticked and why my family behaved as they did was always there. I just needed the motivation and, it seemed, at the age of thirty I suddenly had it: an identity crisis coupled with unemployment!

I will admit, also, that there was another driving factor. My grandfather, Naseeb. For many, many years he had longed to see the old country one more time and had hoped that one of his children might take him. I made a promise to him that I would be the one. While he never mentioned that promise in the years that led up to our journey, he would sit in his chair in the corner of the room and somehow I knew it was in the back of his mind. We had a deal. One that I was determined to honour.

So I assembled the crew. Owing to the complete lack of funding, that crew involved myself and my wife, Nicola, whose holiday pay and the sale of my beloved Ducati paid for the pilot episode. Then a chance meeting with a casual acquaintance, Dave Kelly, was the beginning of something very special indeed.

Dave had gone into business with another friend, David Rudder, to form Espresso Digital, a post-production facility. I needed someone to shoot the series. Someone great, someone with an eye for beautiful pictures, someone who would fit in and tolerate our lack of experience and, most importantly, someone who owned a video camera. I really believe that certain relationships are just meant to be, that you connect with certain people in your life because someone else is pulling the strings. My meeting with Dave Kelly is one of those times.

Over the past two years, Nicola, Dave, his wife Joanna (who has since joined the team as photographer) and I have shared the most extraordinary experiences of our lives. We have travelled the globe (economy class) and seen the kinds of things that you don't get from a tourist brochure. We have been present during pivotal moments in people's lives and we have seen things that none of us will ever forget. These circumstances have created a working family of our own. A close-knit group that includes all of those well-known Australians and their families with whom we travelled. They are no longer professional associations, they are now our friends, largely because of the things we have seen and done together.

Dave: For me *The Ties That Bind* started with a chance meeting with Eden. 'I'm doing a show where well-known Australians with an overseas heritage go back to discover their roots,' he said. I was hooked. 'You wanna shoot it?' I was hired.

At that early stage there was no production schedule and no funding, yet Eden had no doubt whatsoever that this program would be made, or at least he didn't appear to. Here was someone who possessed the imagination and creativity to dream up such a brilliant and simple concept for a TV show, as well as the business savvy to make it a reality. I was quickly drawn in by his enthusiasm for the project. As a Welsh immigrant whose parents brought me to Australia when I was three, it related to my life and to my family as it did to his.

I am one of millions of Australians who owe a debt of gratitude for my lifestyle to the courage and hard work of our parents and grandparents. The choices that they made to come to Australia seem simple enough; some came for financial opportunity, some to escape persecution, others for a better standard of living and health. Quite often we fail to appreciate the pain and sadness that many migrants endured in order to realise these dreams for their families. Having to say goodbye to parents that they knew they would never see again. Having to leave behind everything that was familiar to them. Arriving in a strange land with nothing and starting their lives all over again.

The idea of *The Ties That Bind* which interested me so much was that it was not simply about these migrants' stories, but about how my generation connects with them, relating to where we came from by simply going there and seeing for ourselves. To be present on these journeys, and to be responsible for capturing them on camera was an incredible privilege.

As far as my own migrant experience goes, I am fully aware that my family's journey was made easier by the fact that we came from an English-speaking country with a similar culture to that of Australia. My parents certainly didn't face the same barriers of language, custom or appearance that some of the subjects in our series did. What they did face, however, were all the challenges of leaving their lives behind and starting again in a new country. Through my experiences with *The Ties That Bind* I have gained a greater knowledge of the hardships faced by all immigrants who arrive on our shores for the first time, and therefore a greater appreciation of my own family's story.

The Ties That Bind has been the most satisfying and fulfilling chapter of our lives to date. We doubt that it will be topped. The reasons are there to see in the series, but they are also the moments throughout the journey that were not seen. The ones either not captured on tape or that we had to sacrifice in the final cut. There are also personal reasons. The lessons we have learned and, indeed, the new identity we have gained from our journeying to the birthplace of our ancestors. The funny thing is that it's not something that hits you in the face the minute you step off the plane. The effect of such a journey can only be felt over time through experiences and realisations that occur as a result of that journey. So the pages ahead are the next chapter in *The Ties That Bind*. Personal accounts of how these friends now feel about their journey with that all-important benefit . . . time.

With love and thanks to: Brian Walsh, Ross Crowley, Peter Meakin, Joanna Kelly, David Rudder, Brendan O'Brien, Meredith Brown, Franco di Chiera, Martin Guinness, Gary Grant, Nanette Fox, STA Travel and The National Council for the Centenary of Federation. Special thanks to our families and those families who shared with us their personal stories, to the incredible Selwa Anthony for making this book a reality and to the wonderful Nicola Gaha . . . always an inspiration!

Introduction

Life is becoming more homogenised by the second. There are McDonald's outlets in Moscow, KFCs in Korea and somewhere in the Congo a young African teenager is wearing a Los Angeles Lakers' jersey. Australia hasn't escaped this net. Our culture, attitudes and even our language are being increasingly overtaken by this trend towards North American sameness.

That's not so surprising considering Australia has been one big cultural sponge since European settlement, but what makes us unique and perhaps even a little resistant to sameness is that we've had so many cultures from which to sponge. Mass culture can spread its blanket as far as it likes, but in Australia our identity as individuals and as a nation has been shaped by cultural diversity. We are by no means perfect, but we have been arguably one of the most successful and harmonious multicultural societies on the planet. This is something of which we should be proud and perhaps it is something worth attempting to preserve in the face of globalisation and, indeed, in trying times for international relations.

In a nation now made up mostly of immigrants who have come here from all corners of the earth, the personal identity of many Australians is still tied to the distant places from which their ancestors have come. But

Australia is a long way from almost everywhere and most of us remain isolated from ancestral lands. Despite the speed and ease of travel these days, you can't necessarily just hop on a plane to visit the remote village in which your mother grew up or the pub where your grandfather drank a pint or two with his mates.

It is this very isolation, however, that has seen many Australians make an effort to hold on to a sense of individual cultural heritage. These efforts have greatly enriched us all – we can witness the benefits every day in the glorious diversity of our food, music, art. Naturally, as time goes on and new generations are born, we move a little further away from the past, and the significance of our heritage moves a little further into the background. But as sameness has begun to encroach upon our sense of identity and individuality, something extraordinary seems to have happened: for many, seeking out their family roots has become a priority.

Knowing where you have come from is integral to finding out who you are and more people than ever before are making pilgrimages to the homelands of past generations to satiate their hunger for personal knowledge. And so, as detrimental as globalisation and homogenisation seems, these forces have acted as a kind of catalyst for people to explore or reconnect with the past; to reaffirm family bonds in order to fully understand just where and how they fit into this world.

This book's genesis began late in 2001 when I attended the launch of a unique and timely television documentary series, *The Ties That Bind*. Conceived by actor Eden Gaha to mark the Centenary of Federation for

Foxtel's History Channel, it chronicled the journeys of six well-known Australians to their family's country of origin. Many had never visited their homeland before and others were returning to reconnect with the past after almost a lifetime away. The series traced Eden's own very moving odyssey to Lebanon with his grandfather, then followed in the footsteps of actor and writer Mary Coustas to Greece with her mother and brother; Jay Laga'aia to Samoa with his mother and his young son; Doctor Cindy Pan and her mother to China; rugby league star Craig Wing and his mother as she returned home to the Philippines; and singer Wendy Matthews to Canada to reunite with her family.

Some of their reunions were confronting, but all held moments of unexpected joy. And all proved to be profound journeys of discovery that unlocked secrets of identity and belonging, and helped to heighten the participants' understanding of themselves.

I was so moved by these powerful and inspiring stories that I wept shamelessly through the whole thing. It wasn't just the emotional aspects of family reunion and witnessing the fulfilment of long-held dreams that affected me, it was the revelations of self-discovery that touched me deepest. When I talked to Eden about it, it was clear that this was what had driven him to create such an extraordinary work. The decision that started it all – his initial, tentative step to go to Lebanon – was more than just a wish to fulfil his grandfather's dream of returning. It was a crucial step in Eden's own life search.

Eden's passion was infectious. The idea that I might turn these very personal pilgrimages into a book began to form in my mind. After watching the individual tales unfold on screen, there was a great deal more I wanted to know. The journeys unlocked so much, but for the many questions they answered, they raised many more for me. Of course, there's only a certain amount you can reveal in a half hour of film but each piece offered a tantalising glimpse of a much bigger picture. I wanted to know about the stories and the people behind the scenes: what had inspired these sons and daughters to make this journey of a lifetime to their family's homeland and, just as importantly, what impact did these pilgrimages have on both generations?

For me this book would also turn out to be an opportunity to rediscover my own passion. As a journalist I'd done a lot of celebrity interviewing in my career. I'd spent two years in Los Angeles chatting to everyone from Madonna to Julia Roberts to Denzel Washington to Courtney Love. I had become used to the game and no longer expected full disclosure from people in the public eye. That was just the way it was. But seeing *The Ties That Bind* documentaries and watching those six prominent Australians so candidly and honestly bare their souls, their emotional baggage, their surprising backgrounds and their hearts . . . all this reminded me of why I'd become a writer in the first place: to tell stories in the hope that they would enrich others in some way. That might sound a bit lofty, but really it was a simple matter of being able to do something I believed was truly worthwhile.

When I first started piecing these stories together on paper, I began to search for what it was that connected with me so personally – what was my link to these yarns? I knew they had moved me emotionally, but I didn't seem to have any cultural connection outside Australia to compare to those in the stories. I'd never felt different, or as though there was some piece of me missing, I'd never suffered racism. I am an Aussie, a 'skip', descended from mostly Irish many generations ago. Although I was made very aware that we were of Irish stock by my mum and dad, I was never compelled to trace my roots or dig around for family history beyond the immediate. Us Irish Australians are a dime a dozen, right?

But as I continued to delve into the stories and the book took shape, an incredible journey began for me as a writer and a person. Following in the footsteps of these people as they made their way to far off lands made me eager to find out more about my heritage, to trace my family tree. To find out more about my late father's war service as a gunner for the air force in World War Two and an officer in Korea. And to finally go to Ireland. So what if we're a dime a dozen? It made me realise that I had my own quest for belonging, and it was as valid as the next guy's.

What I discovered was that, yes, I come from a place called Ringwood in Victoria, but that's not the end of the story – not even a patch on the beginning of it. I come from Ringwood, by way of Tasmania, by way of Ireland and a little by way of England. There's some American in there somewhere. My late mother swore there was also some French and some Chinese. I might *look* Irish, and this is the heritage with which I identify most strongly, but just like all those who took part in *The Ties That Bind* documentary series, I am an Australian and very proud of it. But that doesn't mean I can't benefit from knowing where my people originate.

The notion of where we come from is not just one place name; not for any of us. Homeland is not a finite thing: it is living, breathing and as big as the universe. And it links us all.

But what makes it personal, what creates each of our individual stories, is family. Without family, place becomes hollow, just a dot on a map with no emotional terrain to it. Family ties hold strong our sense of identity and individuality and enrich us, like colourful patches on a well-loved quilt. The layers and layers of experience of those who have travelled before us are a fundamental part of who we are, and when we return to their lands we are returning to ourselves. No amount of global sameness will ever break these bonds or diminish our need to feel them. And this book is a celebration of that.

I returned and then everything cleared in my mind.

There were no more clouds.

My spirit was no longer confused.

I was with myself and that was enough.

KALIL GIBRAN

Eden Gaha
Lebanese Australian

Lebanon

The Paris of the Middle East

'I grew up watching the Lebanese killing each other every night on the six o'clock news. But my family kept telling me it was a beautiful country . . .'

Eden Gaha was about to travel to a country he had never been before, but a place that had lived large in his imagination all his life: Lebanon. With him he would be taking precious cargo: his ninety-four-year-old grandfather, Naseeb, who had left his home in Lebanon seventy-five years ago. In Lebanon Eden would finally fulfil a promise to his grandfather to take him back to Bechmezzine, the village in which he grew up.

This pilgrimage of grandfather and grandson would be captured forever on film as Eden was going to make a documentary about the experience. Having made a living out of show business all his adult life, Eden was used to being in front of a camera, but this was more real and personal than anything he had ever done before in his career. It was a trip both he and Naseeb needed to make: Eden to see his family's homeland for the first time and his grandfather to return after almost a lifetime away.

It was also uncharted territory in other ways. Though Eden had been constantly in the public eye for over a decade – he had been a TV reporter, starred in big production musicals, had done stints on television in soaps, series and game shows, and even performed Shakespeare at the Opera House – he had never made a documentary before.

Eden's success as an actor wasn't all that surprising, given that performing was in his blood. His dad, Anthony Gaha, was a musician, performer and theatrical producer, and his mother, Janice Breen, was a performer, choreographer and dance teacher; his sister, Dannielle, a talented singer. Even his grandfather, Naseeb, had dabbled in acting, having appeared in the 1941 Australian classic, *40,000 Horsemen*.

Eden had inherited dark good looks from his father and grandfather. He couldn't look in a mirror without being reminded that he was Lebanese. But for others it was a look that was hard to pin as Arabic. He could just as easily have been Spanish. Or Italian. Or Irish for that matter, which he was by half. His look fitted no stereotype. At school, the Anglo kids had seen it differently and much more simplistically: he was a wog. But in his adult years, his exotic good looks had worked for him, though, of course, it also helped that he was a good bloke and a versatile talent. Add to that a beautiful and equally talented wife, a loving family, and Eden Gaha had it all.

But good looks, personality and acting talent had little to do with the journey on which he was about to embark – or his ability as a documentary maker. He'd sold his beloved motorbike, and his wife Nicola had cashed in her holiday pay to finance this trip – the bags were packed and the camera was ready to roll. Eden, Nicola and Naseeb were going to Lebanon. And they were taking with them a cameraman, David Kelly, who was going to record every moment on video.

The seed of this journey to Lebanon had begun to sprout in 1999.

That year Nicola, also an accomplished performer, landed a dream job in the musical *Chicago*, and had to move from Sydney to Melbourne to take up the role. Eden was thrilled for her despite the fact that the two of them had spent more time apart than together since marrying earlier that year and this would mean another separation. Only three weeks after the ceremony, Eden had to join the cast of the stage comedy *Wogboys*, in Wollongong, while Nicola remained in Sydney for her own work. After weekends together and a brief full-time reunion in Sydney, Nicola had gone to Melbourne for *Chicago* while Eden finished a Sydney run of the stage musical *Leader of the Pack*. Such is life when both partners are not only performers, but performers in work. They have to go where the work is because they never know when it might run out – as Eden was about to find out.

After *Leader of the Pack* wound up, Eden joined Nicola in Melbourne to enjoy what he thought would be a brief break from his own work. But as he sipped champagne at the premiere party for *Chicago* and toasted Nicola's success, little did he know he was also toasting the beginning of one of the most confronting periods of his life.

Eden's phone did not ring, at least not with offers of gigs, for six months. Alone in the couple's serviced apartment, the walls began closing in. There is only so much café coffee you can drink, only so many hours you can spend in the gym, a limit to how many kilometres a day you should run. 'I'm a control freak and I like to be doing something all the time,' said Eden. 'I was being a real pain in the ass. I was driving Nicola nuts. There was nothing to do.'

Nothing, except tinker on the Internet and think.

It began with thoughts of his identity. Left alone, without his work, the single thing that had defined his sense of self more than any other, old questions about who he was, found space to come to the fore. And then his mind turned to thoughts of his grandfather; the promise Eden had made . . .

Gaha family gatherings were always raucous, foody affairs, big personalities vying for the floor, laughter ringing from wall to wall. In the middle of this happy chaos Naseeb, or Ubbi (pronounced 'ah-bih', the Arabic word for 'father') as Eden affectionately called him, would hold court. In his nineties, Naseeb was still handsome and elegant, a kerchief tucked neatly and stylishly under his black crewneck jumper, his silver hair tied back in a sleek ponytail and the facial bone structure that had led to comparisons to Omar Sharif in his earlier days still holding. Though his cane was by his side and his once strong body had weakened with age, the power of his personality, his love and humour had not diminished. But his physical capabilities clearly had, and occasionally he forgot things. He wasn't getting any younger.

Sometimes, in quiet moments, Ubbi's eyes betrayed a longing, his thoughts would drift into memories of long ago and he would talk of Lebanon, of returning once more to his village of beloved Bechmezzine. One day. One last time.

'We should take him back to Lebanon,' Eden had said at one such family gathering. Nicola had agreed. But like other family members who had vowed to accompany their beloved patriarch on his pilgrimage, Eden and Nicola's good intention had been swamped by their busy lives. They'd talk of their idea every now and then. *We really must. Yes, we must.* And then Eden's agent would ring or Nicola would get a show.

Now, a year on, alone in the silent Melbourne apartment, there was nothing standing between Eden and fulfilling his grandfather's dream of returning to Lebanon, save the actor's usual insecurity of wanting to be 'around' in case the big offer came in. The longer the big offer stayed away, the more he thought about that long-postponed excursion.

But there was a problem even the best intentions in the world could seemingly not overcome. Eden was bringing in no income. 'My original thought was: how can I get to Lebanon without having to pay for it?' he admitted.

Life has its ways of leading you where you need to go. As Eden began to explore the possibilities on the Internet, the recurring images of Lebanon and scrawling Arabic script triggered old memories. He began to read piles of travel books and brochures, and then moved on to weightier historical tomes. The dichotomies he uncovered about Lebanon – heyday and war, glamour and devastation – stirred up his old personal conundrum of identity. These images seemed so foreign and familiar all at the same time and he submerged himself in them.

The more he discovered, the more questions it raised: *Who are you? Where do you come from? Who are your people? What does it mean to be Lebanese? What does it mean to be Australian? Who are you?* Eden's usually perfect show business veneer began to crack, allowing the ghosts of childhood to rise up and engulf him. 'I started looking inward and got very depressed about who I was and what my identity was,' he said.

Was he Lebanese at all? His Lebanese father, born in Australia, had never set foot in the land of his forebears.

Eden's parents had separated when he was very young, and he had been brought up under his mother's Irish Catholic roof. What did that make him?

Eden had not thought about these issues for many years. He hadn't had the time. His career had been on acceleration since he was in his mid-teens. He'd had no need to look back or to question his identity. In high school he'd discovered his talent for being the class clown and, feeling that his quickness to banter was his best asset, he'd abandoned serious study and set his sights on a career in radio. Barely seventeen, he scored an interview at Sydney's 2DAY FM for the job of office boy. It was in the days when the answers to the questions 'Are you a Catholic?' and 'Who's your father?' were the clinchers. As a Catholic whose old man was well connected in the world of showbiz, Eden was soon in and on his way, far away from the picked-on, woggy-looking kid in the schoolyard.

'I had this gift of the gab,' said Eden. 'I didn't know where it came from. I guess it came from my old man who is also very talented in that regard. Even though he wasn't around that much to influence me in my childhood, maybe it was in the genes I got from him.'

The gift had propelled him far away from any schoolyard jibes or questions about how he fitted in. But as he sat there researching Lebanon it all came flooding back.

He remembered that feeling of alienation he'd experienced throughout his schooldays. He began to see himself back there, a child who had fallen through the cracks of belonging. 'I started thinking about how I grew up in school looking like a wog but not really being one. I had this sense of looking like an Arab, being brought up an Irish Catholic in a very Australian, Anglo household. And in the schoolyard that meant I looked like a wog, but I wasn't one, so I fell between the gaps. I wasn't in the group that were the wogs because I didn't speak a second language and I didn't really understand their mannerisms. Yet the skips, the Australians, saw me as just another wog. So I would drift between the groups, never really settling in.'

The private Sydney school he attended was no different to any other school. It had its group of outcasts, and Eden gravitated towards them. But throughout his school years there was one place where he was king. Every Monday night Eden would catch a glimpse of Lebanon when he stayed with his grandmother Margaret and his grandfather Naseeb at their home in Coogee. 'He waited on me hand and foot,' recalled Eden. It was his only taste of Lebanese life, and then only through the food and the accents and the occasional showing of photographs. He never asked, nor was he ever told, the stories of how his grandparents arrived in Australia. 'We wouldn't really talk about Lebanon. We'd watch *Sale of the Century* together.'

Eden's grandparents were proud to call themselves Australian and had worked hard to assimilate. They had forsaken outward expressions of the old country, having arrived in pre-World War Two Sydney at a time when 'wog' was not an Australian term of endearment, not in any quarter. Ethnic differences were not celebrated and they knew only of the difficulties of being 'other' in a land dominated by Anglo–Saxon and Celtic white skin. Though they relied on their fellow Lebanese nationals for a sense of connection and community, they hoped to make it easier for their children by concentrating on English and 'Waltzing Matilda'. And their children, with no trace of a foreign accent, no Lebanese soil on their shoes, had hoped to make it even easier for theirs. It had seemed to Eden that the only thing that had never been forsaken in his grandparents' efforts to assimilate was the cuisine.

Growing up, Eden would catch snippets of the stories behind the photographs of his grandfather and grandmother, his great aunts and uncles, when they were young. Looking at those images he could see a glimmer of the proud place Lebanon used to be.

'I grew up watching the Lebanese killing each other every night on the six o'clock news. But my family kept telling me it was a beautiful country, the people are friendly,' Eden said. 'They told me it was the Paris of the Middle East. There was fruit growing on every tree.' But even when the fighting had stopped and Lebanon was on the slow path of healing and regeneration, the negative images of his seventies childhood resonated for him. He'd felt somehow ashamed to be connected to a land that had seen so much war, a land from which people wanted to escape.

Now, as an adult facing the dilemma of who he was and where he'd come from, Eden didn't really know how he felt about Lebanon, except that he needed to hear

Naseeb talk of this country, to know who those people in the photos were and to see this place for himself. 'I wanted to go to Lebanon for the first time and I wanted to share it with my closest Lebanese connection – and that connection was my grandfather.'

But Naseeb was now ninety-four. Did they let ninety-four-year-olds on overseas flights? Could he make such a long journey? Would his health hold out? These were serious concerns. And how would he cope emotionally? Naseeb hadn't been back to the old country since 1974, his only visit after emigrating in 1926. The Lebanon of Naseeb's mind was an almost fabled homeland now. Was it responsible of Eden to expose that to fallibility? In 1974 Beirut was still the Paris of the Middle East, but in 1975 civil war broke out, and conflict after conflict ravaged the country until the early nineties. Much of the once-beautiful capital had been destroyed and more than 150,000 people had been killed. A trip back might well be worse than Naseeb passing away without seeing his home again. At least then his gilded memories would remain untarnished.

For years, a succession of family members had promised to take Naseeb to Lebanon. No one had done it. And all of a sudden, Eden reckoned he was the one to do it. Eden, who didn't speak a word of Arabic and whose exposure to Lebanese culture had been pretty much limited to Monday night dinners cooked by Naseeb and Margaret.

Quiet doubts set in. Eden had never really felt Lebanese. If it was a sojourn to the homeland he was after, he may as well have taken the 373 bus to Sydney's

Coogee beach. It was at Coogee that, as a kid, he used to spend those Monday nights with his granddad and get spoiled rotten. And it was at Coogee that his mum had a dance studio and gave young Eden his first taste for what essentially was the family business – performing.

He remembered happy times at Coogee but he only remembered being embarrassed about Lebanon. And confused. What was he trying to achieve with this idea of going back to Lebanon: was it about Ubbi, or himself?

Nicola was worried about Eden's brooding, but she could empathise to some degree. She knew something about feelings of displacement. Having migrated from New Zealand, Nicola had lived away from her family for over a decade. The move had paid off; life had led her where she needed to go. She went back to New Zealand when she could, but work and then love had taken her away and kept her beyond home. Distance could have diminished the importance of family and roots but, for Nicola, it did quite the opposite. The importance of family came into focus, her origins became the touch-stone for her sense of self. So when Eden began to realise that his own sense of self was murky to say the least, she had no hesitation in encouraging him to delve further. In fact, she was eager to be involved.

It was with a free passage to Lebanon in his sights that Eden came up with the idea of making a documentary. 'I was pigheaded enough to think making a documentary about myself would be interesting and that somebody would pay for it,' he said. 'That's where the education in Australian television production began.'

The planned documentary's credits didn't look too promising. Eden, as producer, was a proven on-air talent, but far from proven behind the scenes. Nicola, as researcher and sound operator, was likewise a great talent, but she'd done neither of these jobs before. Then there was the star of the show: a ninety-four-year-old man of great presence but few words. Dave, the cameraman, who moonlighted in Russell Crowe's rock band '30 Odd Foot of Grunts', was the only one with any real credentials. Dave and Eden had met through work a few years earlier and, when Eden ran into his old colleague by chance one day, he had told Dave about his documentary idea and asked, 'You wanna shoot it?' Dave, the son of Welsh immigrants, jumped at the chance. He'd always wanted to travel to the Middle East and what's more he agreed to work without pay; going along for the ride, the experience and the inspiration.

Unfortunately, despite their enthusiasm, no one in the TV industry was inspired. Getting a doco up is a bit like going for a loan at the bank. You can be the nicest person in the world with the best reason for needing money, but if the credentials don't add up on paper, forget it.

It became clear that no one was going to pay for Eden's documentary. But Eden had gone too far down the path to turn back. He would pay for the trip himself. After all this time thinking, planning, delving into issues that had lain dormant for all those years, a new kind of energy took hold – Eden's need for freedom from the burden of not knowing: not knowing if Lebanon meant anything to him. There was a big, empty chasm in his self-knowledge. He needed to fill it.

The professional and financial risks Eden was taking were nothing compared to the personal. And the greatest risk, it seemed, involved that precious cargo, Naseeb. Naseeb was many things to many people. He was Eden's Ubbi, but he was also his large, close family's Ubbi. And then he was also Naseeb, somewhat of a personality in the Sydney Lebanese community. He and his wife Margaret had been the belles of the ball at any social gathering in their heyday. They loved to dance. They didn't do so much of it these days but their popularity had not diminished. Naseeb was the cantor in his church, a respected member of the southern Sydney Lebanese community and a friend to many.

Eden was acutely aware of his responsibility and so was relieved when Naseeb's physician, Doctor Casamento, gave Naseeb a thorough check up and declared him fit to travel. But Naseeb didn't really care what Doctor Casamento said. Two weeks before his flight was due to take off, he'd already packed his suitcase. 'Very excited . . . very excited,' he kept saying over and over again like a mantra.

For the sake of his documentary, Eden wanted Naseeb to say more than 'very excited', but for Naseeb, the statement encompassed everything he was capable of expressing and everything he was not. He was indeed in a state of high excitement. This trip meant so much to him and for so many reasons that he did not know where to begin to expand upon it. Nevertheless he tried.

'I think of myself as Australian. I have forgotten my Lebanese nationality,' Naseeb said to Eden and laughed. But later, his gaze grew distant, the laughter gave way to a quiver in his voice, and he spoke of his village in Lebanon. 'It is beautiful there. The people are beautiful there. I love Bechmezzine.'

The day before leaving for Lebanon, Naseeb and Margaret hosted a big slap-up Lebanese lunch for the family in their large, cosy, red velvet and dark wood furnished flat above Coogee Bay Road. Naseeb had prepared Eden's favourite: *kibbeh nayye*, a traditional Lebanese dish of raw lamb and cracked wheat mixed together and served like steak tartare. 'It takes a real Leb to enjoy it,' Eden joked, although he felt anything but a real Lebanese that day.

Children and adults gathered around the table, Naseeb at the head as always. Before them lay mountains of tabouleh, flat bread and dips. The apartment smelled of lemons and garlic, parsley and spice. Family members kissed each other on the cheek three times, the Lebanese greeting. But Eden still did not feel Lebanese. And he did not dare to allow himself to think of the uncharted emotional territory into which he was heading.

'I hoped it was either going to make me understand being Lebanese more or it was going to make me more Australian. Maybe I would realise: You know what? I *am* Australian. And that would be perfectly valid. To think: I've moved on from my grandparents' life and I'm okay with that. I didn't care what the reaction was going to be. I just wanted there to be a reaction, and my biggest fear was having no reaction; going, "So what?" and not feeling anything at all.'

Inspired by the occasion, Naseeb expanded a little on 'very excited' that afternoon, acknowledging that many of the friends and family he'd known back in Bechmezzine would have passed on now; 'But I'll see their children,' he nodded, tapping his cane, determined to look on the positive side.

At lunch, Eden listened intently as his Uncle Neville told him: 'You'll want to talk Arabic to somebody and as soon as you feel good and are about to say, *kifak* – how are you? – they'll talk to you in French. Everybody speaks French and English.'

Eden was not sure there would be a moment where he'd want to speak to someone in Arabic, but he was glad the word 'English' was included in his uncle's advice.

After the meal, he laughed with his siblings, teased his nieces and nephews, and clapped along, somewhat amazed, when some of his family members broke into Lebanese song to mark the occasion. 'This is too weird. My family never sings after lunch,' he laughed. But what else might a showbiz family do when the spotlight lands firmly on their Lebaneseness? Sing a Lebanese song, of course.

Eden could really only look on with bemusement; he did not know the song, he did not understand it, but perhaps he understood something of the energy in the gesture. It seemed a small validation of him being on the right path.

At the airport, reality began to set in. Family had come to see them off and as the Gaha men put reassuring hands on Eden and Naseeb's shoulders, the quiet was an extension of what Naseeb couldn't say. They were all bursting with anticipation. But very worried as well.

Naseeb finally showed the layers below 'very excited'. He wept. Eden hugged him hard, trying not to cry himself. And when his Ubbi, pulling his handkerchief from his pocket and wiping his eyes like a little boy, said softly, his voice breaking, 'I am not good saying goodbye,' Eden knew that his grandfather had considered the notion that this might be his final farewell.

'If anything happens to me while I am there with you,' Naseeb had said to Eden the day before, 'bury me with my father. You hear?' Naseeb had laughed as he said it and Eden had laughed along and promised to do as he requested. But in his mind, the promise was no laughing matter. It was a promise Eden prayed he wouldn't have cause to keep.

In Kuala Lumpur, their final stop before Lebanon, Eden and Nicola went to change money, leaving Naseeb seated in the transit lounge with Dave the cameraman.

There was a large TV screen in the lounge showing motorcross racing, and Naseeb and Dave sat watching it, in a silence that went for too long and made Dave uncomfortable. Finally Naseeb took pity on him. He suddenly motioned with a flourish of his hand to the riders on the screen flying through the air as their bikes hit dirt mounds.

'They are very daring,' he said in his slow, deliberate way.

Though the suddenness and edictal nature of Naseeb's pronouncement made Dave want to laugh, he couldn't help but agree. Daring, he thought, was an old-fashioned word, but a word that nailed its meaning precisely. As the man who would be watching Naseeb through a camera lens, he realised then that Naseeb would always be a man of few words, but he was very 'daring' himself, allowing Dave to follow him with a camera on his journey to Bechmezzine, into what was obviously deeply emotional terrain.

At their next stop, Dubai, in the United Arab Emirates, Naseeb could hear the Arabic and smell the smells of a different world. The light was *that* light, the light in his dreams. The air, hot and dry, was something fundamental to his senses. After all these years, he was only a flight away. Just a few hours' flight over Saudi Arabia and he would be in Lebanon. And within days, he would be in Bechmezzine. He felt even more impatient.

This stopover was just an obstacle in his way to getting there.

It was over ten years since the war in Lebanon had ended, but even from the air, flying into Beirut in 1999, the city's wounds were startling. It was a small city in area, but great tracts of it were devoid of buildings, trees, anything but apricot-coloured dust, reminding the visitor of the catastrophe that had occurred there. Once hostilities had stopped, the Beirutis had, as quickly and efficiently as possible, bulldozed the many sites where the devastation was irreversible. They had sought to clear away the remnants of war and make a fresh start.

If you had asked a Beirut native then, they would no doubt have said that a remarkable transformation had taken place. Four years of the planned five-year rebuilding of the city was almost complete. Basic infrastructure had been repaired, buildings that could be salvaged had mostly been restored, and Beirut's restaurants and bars were full of optimistic locals intent on celebrating the future.

But for Eden, looking out of the plane window at the scarred city below – whole blocks of dirt nothingness, not even rubble – Beirut appeared more like a land gashed by open-cut mining than a cosmopolitan Mediterranean city. He was tired from travel and stressed with thoughts of having invested so much personal money in a documentary that he was not certain anyone would be interested in screening, let alone buying. He worried for his grandfather's physical and emotional health. Eden had come seeking answers, but now, faced with the reality of shortly landing in Lebanon, gazing over the ugly, motley freshness of Beirut's wounds, he was fearful of finding them. Before they'd even hit the ground here was the proof of his childhood perceptions, hard evidence backing up all those years of seeing Lebanon's troubles played out on the television news.

'To me, the Lebanese had been these people who ran backwards and who couldn't defend themselves and were hopeless, fighting over ridiculous things,' said Eden. 'I wasn't very proud to be a Leb. In fact, I was genuinely embarrassed to be Lebanese.'

Things did not get better on the ground. Eden's aesthetic sense jarred; he just didn't connect to this city in any way. All he saw was mayhem. There were no immediately obvious traces of Beirut's ancient history. It was grimy and claustrophobic, as far as Eden was concerned. There was nothing for him to latch on to. Nothing that spoke to him as a Lebanese man. Or as an Australian.

Lebanon itself is about the size of the greater Sydney area, 10,452 square kilometres. It takes only three hours to drive from its northernmost tip to its southernmost – where Lebanon meets Israel, and where occupying Israeli SLA militia, Palestinians and the Lebanese Hezbollah fighters clashed until the Israelis withdrew in May 2000. Because of the troubles down south most rebuilding had taken place in the north. With three million people, Lebanon is one of the world's most densely populated countries, and half Lebanon's population live in Beirut, a land area of only sixty-seven square kilometres.

For Eden, the city was depressing, dismal: 'Beirut was full of dust, it was bullet riddled, people drove like maniacs, it was noisy, it was hot, crowded. It wasn't very appealing. I hated it. Nicola and I would get back to the place where we were staying and go, "Ah shit, the food isn't as good as my grandmother makes it, everything's crowded." There was a sense of manic oppression in the city.'

The legacy of war

Naseeb wasn't too interested in Beirut either. He was tired and clearly yearning to get back to Bechmezzine.

He was in Lebanon now and the familiarity was excruciating. So close, and yet so far. For Naseeb, the saying was never so poignant. Every moment since their arrival, his love for his village was heavy around him, as if he was wading through the syrup of it.

'I love Bechmezzine,' he had said to Eden before they left. 'I love Bechmezzine people. I never forget Bechmezzine. I have always thought of Bechmezzine and going back. I remember *everything*. I have very beautiful memories . . .'

Before leaving for Bechmezzine, though, Eden and Naseeb would first meet up with Naseeb's wife's niece, Lilly, and her husband, Edmund. For Eden this first meeting with extended family was quite a surprise. 'They were genuinely excited that we were there. They're cousins twice or three times removed, and yet they treat you like they're your uncle or brother,' said Eden. 'They're just so happy to have someone with the same surname who happens to be from the same lineage in their presence, and they treat you like absolute royalty. That's a Lebanese thing. And it was also the fact that Ubbi was so old. Age gives you a degree of royalty in Lebanon.'

Eden immediately began calling them Uncle Edmund and Aunty Lilly. 'It was a real eye opener to me about how important family could be,' he said. 'I think in Western society we've become very detached from the idea of extended family and we have become obsessed with immediate family. To them anybody with the same surname is regarded as highly as father, mother, brother, sister, and considering the turmoil the country's been through perhaps that's because that is all they have. It's like a clan. A tribal thing.'

The next day, as the Gahas pulled their hire car into a parking lot, they were amazed that it was run by an Australian company. 'It was like they'd just levelled a few bomb sites around Beirut and had done nothing else to the sites except put parking attendants there,' said Dave. The tenuous link of an Australian parking lot gave them an idea: maybe there was someone there who could speak English. While their Lebanese itinerary was well-planned, things would be easier if they had an English and Arabic-speaking guide, driver and interpreter at their disposal. They had been discussing this with Edmund and Lilly, neither of whom could fill the role due to work commitments. So Eden enlisted his Uncle Edmund to ask the parking attendant whether he knew anyone who spoke English and who could act as a guide and driver. The parking attendant, Johnny, volunteered for the job without hesitation.

This was not such an uncommon thing in Beirut. Traveller stories abounded of tourists being taken under the wing of Beirutis keen to make sure visitors had a good time – and got to see the Beirut of which they were proud, rather than just the vestiges of war. They wanted tourists to take their stories from Beirut to the rest of the world, to show that they were neither terrorists nor hopelessly war weary, but a cosmopolitan people on the verge of new affluence and a new era.

The following day, while Naseeb stayed behind to receive guests as if he were indeed royalty, Johnny picked up Eden, Nicola and Dave in his big old black Mercedes Benz. He took them on a tour of the redeveloped central business district, the archeological remains of Roman times, which had been uncovered after the razing of bombed buildings, as well as the oasis-green campus of the American University, the Middle East's most prestigious seat of learning.

Eden, however, was finding it difficult to get beyond the stark evidence of the civil war, particularly along the Green Line that once separated Muslim West Beirut from the Christian East. 'It was just too confronting to ignore despite obvious efforts of the proud Lebanese people to sweep it under the carpet,' he said.

The old Green Line was still a sorry sight. The remaining buildings along the former buffer zone looked diseased rather than damaged, so repetitive was the injury: layers and layers of pock marks, chunks missing everywhere. Concrete lepers. The years of Muslim–Christian discord inflamed by the force of French, American, Syrian, Israeli, Iranian and Palestinian interests merging in the one tiny place were still clearly evident.

Dave was fascinated and of course wanted to capture these scenes on film. But the Beirutis didn't like it. 'Why do you want to take pictures of such ugliness? Photograph our new buildings. Photograph the lovely high rises that are being built,' Johnny said. Others, particularly police and soldiers, actually prevented Dave from shooting the evidence of war. He soon found out that it was also unacceptable to attempt to photograph any of the military checkpoints throughout Lebanon.

'Dave and I tried to get a shot of a military check-point,' said Eden, 'but it scared the shit out of us; just the attempt. These guys were no older than us and had probably never fired a gun, but when Dave brought out the camera, they pointed at us and tapped on their machine guns. And when someone's got one hand on a machine gun and the other pointing at you, you know they're not going to shoot you but you just don't want to end up in a room somewhere being interrogated, with the tape ripped out of the camera.'

As the producer of this documentary in the making, Eden found the interference from the police and military frustrating, but he was also becoming frustrated with himself. With three roles to play – producer, director and reporter – he was finding it impossible to connect with his feelings for the place. 'It was tough, really tough, trying to step outside the production roles I was playing and be real and honest about it,' he said.

Standing there on the Green Line, he might have paused to process the sorrow for Lebanon that had built up inside him from all those childhood TV news broadcasts. But he didn't. Dave shot the action as Eden, his million-dollar smile in place, attempted to run across the intense bedlam the Beirutis call traffic along the Rue de Damas, the road which had demarcated the Green Line during the war. Stopping on the crumbling median strip he looked down the lens, foreign correspondent-style, and proclaimed, 'Once you might have worried about dodging bullets here; now all you have to worry about is getting run over.'

The result was great production footage, but Eden was still craving a real, honest connection with the place, and as it happened Johnny was to be the key.

When Eden expressed his liking for a morning run, Johnny pointed him in the direction of the Corniche. The name Corniche comes from a French word meaning 'ledge' in English, and that was pretty much what it was, or 'Bondi with bullet holes', as Eden described this promenade which runs along the Beirut promontory. It stretches five kilometres from Raouché in the southwest to the St George Yacht Club bordering the downtown district. On the inland side, chic restaurants and cafés line the Corniche, and out to the west, the Mediterranean. As Eden ran, the sunrise cast a glorious golden light along the chalk cliffs lining the Mediterranean and across Pigeon Rocks, Beirut's famed natural arches rising magnificently from the blue below. The scene seemed a powerful reminder of the impermanence of man's actions and the infinity of nature's grandeur. You could wage war, but the sun would still rise and set, and this ancient land would still look beautiful for it. Eden saw the beauty in Beirut then. But he saw it beyond just the postcard perfection of the light.

'It was all about the people,' said Eden. 'When I ran with all the Beirutis along the Corniche, I felt like one of them. I began to enjoy it then. The smell of the air of the Mediterranean, sweating, seeing other people do the same thing, watching the sun rise over the Corniche, I felt like I was clicking into something. I see that as a turning point, a special moment. It didn't involve anyone

I knew; just me, doing something from a human point of view that was very natural.'

Johnny had another treat in store for Eden, one they'd all click into. Though the city boasted (and it did, literally) two Hard Rock Cafés, several McDonald's outlets, New York-style bars and restaurants, as well as many English-style pubs, that night Johnny understood that his charges wanted to see and taste the real Beirut. So, despite his earlier protestations that they should only take in the new and (according to his definition) beautiful, he drove them to a traditional restaurant that was far from the monuments of great natural beauty of the morning. It was plain, sparse and cavernous, its single point of decorative interest a pleated canopy dropping from the ceiling to create a marquee effect. Far more decorative were the patrons. Women dripped with gold jewellery, all big hairdos, gaudy silks in skimpy styles, and high heels. The men in shirt collars and tailored trousers sat at long tables, puffing on the *narghile*, the ancient tobacco pipe of the Middle East. They drank *arak*, the local aniseed beverage, which tasted like ouzo or pernod, but went down more like something NASA would use to fuel a Mars mission. After a dinner of kibbeh and hummus, tabouleh and shwarma, the line between restaurant and nightclub blurred, as it usually did in Beirut restaurants. As live musicians played traditional Arabic music, the men and women danced the *raks sharki*, the men dropping to their knees in balletic worship of their goddesses.

'They were focused on having fun, definitely not taking themselves too seriously . . . perhaps this place isn't so foreign after all,' Eden said, and he and Nicola joined in. As Eden danced he relaxed completely. He was just a bloke dancing with his wife, and in that state his thoughts wandered to his family. He thought of how theatrical his family was, particularly the Gaha men. But looking around the room, he thought his Gahas might have all fitted right in. Then he noticed *he* fitted right in. Apart from the fact that he was dancing with the only fair woman in the place, his features were the rule, not the exception.

'I'd always thought the Gahas lived beyond their means, were flamboyant, vain, were very much into the way things looked and the appearance of wealth. But I discovered then, that trait was typically *Lebanese*. It was not typically *Gaha*. I mean, even my grandfather, he was proud. He had only stopped dyeing his hair a decade earlier and the ponytail – again, the vanity. So it was just so satisfying to find out where these things came from. You can understand more about your own family seeing them in context.'

Eden slept very well that night, and not just because of the sea air and the rocket-fuel *arak*.

Johnny was at the wheel of his big old black Mercedes, attempting a parallel park, with the Gaha party on board, when he scraped the side of a brand new BMW, causing quite a bit of damage. As the owner of the BMW happened to be seated on a fold-out stool on the pavement next to his vehicle, Johnny wound down his window. The two men fired off annoyed statements in Arabic with much hand-gesturing. But annoyed was as far as it got before the BMW owner sat back on his stool and returned to his newspaper. And Johnny drove on. No numbers exchanged, no nothing. It was an absurd, anarchic, but wonderful scene. Few recriminations. Just getting on with it, as Beirutis did in life generally. It was also hilariously comical, and the typically Beiruti display delighted Johnny's passengers.

Soon they were outside the city, heading off on a day trip to the resort town of Zahlé and then on to the ancient ruins of Baalbek. In the back seat Naseeb was giving Eden instruction in the ways of Arabic singing, until his grandson got too cheeky, warbling in an exaggerated imitation, and Naseeb laughingly told him to shut up. Johnny's crazy scrape had put them in a giddy mood, and now their laughter relaxed them all. It felt great. As they motored along, expectations not met or yet to be met, disillusionments and concerns were left far behind.

Even the dry barrenness of the Roman wheatbelt landscape along their northern route could not flag Eden's spirits. He was beginning to think that his experience of Lebanon was going to be much more about people and less about a connection with place than he had anticipated – though that was about to change.

As they travelled due west towards the border with Syria, they reached the Bekaa Valley, where Lebanon's modern agriculture sat squarely next to its ancient history, the remnants left behind by invaders and traders from the time of Christ.

'What I saw was barren land,' said Eden. 'I saw hills that might have once been covered in beautiful cedar trees that over thousands and thousands of years had been cut down and cleared. Whereas my Uncle Edmund said of it, "Isn't the Bekaa Valley absolutely magnificent?" All I could see was a wasteland, but from his point of view it was absolutely beautiful because of the history. That was a real lesson in perspective. It wasn't beautiful in a traditional sense but beautiful from a historical point of view. It took me a while to adjust to that.'

In Zahlé, the Sydney Gahas met up again with Uncle Edmund and Aunty Lilly for a morning stroll and an early lunch. Set along the steep banks of the Birdawni River, the town favoured by Beirutis for weekend escapes has something of the old Lebanon in its bearing. Cobbled streets, Ottoman-era houses, market stalls, women making *marquok* bread, and the smell of tobacco smoking in the *narghile* caused a deep yet still faint stirring in Eden, like the rumbling of a past life. He couldn't say what it was, but soon he would be able to.

Naseeb's remembrances were getting clearer all the time. This place was moving closer to what he knew. The rebuilt Beirut lacked familiarity in many ways, yet it was familiar in so many others. Though impatient still to get to Bechmezzine, in the city Naseeb could enjoy sit-down chats with relatives and the novelty of speaking Arabic. But here, in Zahlé, the taste of the pistachio and sesame sweet called *kahk* sampled from a street vendor, and the

Arabic music from the buskers, made him lift his cane and dance a small jig. He could smell cedar. He could feel the mountain air. And he felt invigorated.

Zahlé was famous for its open-air restaurants along the river, where fine Lebanese cuisine was served with *arak* and the local beer, Almaza. Choosing Almaza over the rocket fuel, Eden's party settled at a long table among many others, each it seemed full of large, happy Lebanese families, just like his party. And just like his family back home. 'It reminded me of being in Coogee at a big long table with all the family eating Lebanese dinner. That was really comfortable for me. I got it. I absolutely got it and so did Nic.'

By afternoon, they had reached Baalbek. Aunty Lilly and Uncle Edmund had timed the trip so that their relatives would be there for sunset. 'It's a must in Lebanon, to see the sun set at Baalbek,' said Edmund.

Eden had already seen some Lebanese sunsets and thought they were the most magnificent in the world. He had heard that the famous complex of temples at Baalbek was among the Seven Wonders of the World. He had read of it as the 'Sun City' of the Roman era, a place the mystically inclined claimed still had great spiritual power. More imposing than anything the Romans had built anywhere else in their world, his research had told him that the nine different places of Roman worship at Baalbek were the most important Roman archeological sites in the Middle East. The main Temple of Jupiter was over three hundred metres long and there you could still see six of the largest ancient columns in the world:

The temples at Baalbek

twenty-three metres high, with a diameter of more than two metres. They were all that remained of a set of fifty-four.

He knew all that. But nothing could have prepared him for the impact of the real thing. 'Its construction began way before the Romans got there,' said Eden. 'It harked back to a time before the Lebanese were even Arabs. Just as the Iranians consider themselves Persians, the Lebanese are very much into the fact that they are Phoenicians. When you see how much has gone on in the land of your ancestors and how much has been achieved there, it makes you realise that they are more than just the guys who ran backwards in the civil war of the 1970s. Baalbek was the beginning of that realisation for me.

'Everybody had been through there – the Crusaders and the Greeks. Not all of these are achievements that the Lebanese themselves can claim because they are a hybrid of all the Greeks, Romans and Turks. But the fact that a particular structure exists in the land of my ancestors and that they probably had a lot to do with its construction makes me feel proud. And the fact that it is still here and intact, despite war and the passage of time, is something to be proud of.'

Though life may well be about an imperfect and inconclusive search for enlightenment, the life of every person consciously seeking some sort of meaning may nonetheless invite complete, perfect moments of clarity. At the temple of Baalbek, the heavens were about to open up in revelation for Eden.

There were no crowds, tour buses or hawkers there, instead, a sense of majesty and peace beckoned him towards the ancient structures.

As he wandered amid soaring columns and carved images of the Roman gods, Diana, Victoria, Fortuna, Vulcan, Bacchus, Cupid and Ceres, and mythical tritons, nereids, gorgons and dragons, he not only felt awestruck but humbled. The sun began to set and the holy stones glowed iridescent orange. Somewhere in the distance an imam called his congregation to prayer, the haunting song of Islam an aural illustration of the spiritual serenity that now filled Eden. And with that serenity came a kind of awakening: for the first time in his life, Eden was proud to be Lebanese.

'Baalbek had made me feel proud of Lebanese achievement. I never thought the Lebanese achieved anything except losing the war, and to see what they achieved before Australian was even a nationality, that was overwhelming.

'And I guess it was a double-edged thing,' said Eden. 'As an Australian, I had also had that common thing of feeling inferior because we're a young nation and because we had always been told that Mother England was the one that we'd love for ever more. We could look up to her, but never really measure up to her. And then, for me being half Irish and half Lebanese, that often had further negative connotations. But all of a sudden I had this amazing connection with an extraordinary history. I felt truly honoured, in a way that defies description.'

It had been a jolly, vocal drive in Johnny's Mercedes Benz out to Baalbek. It was a quiet one back to Beirut, each passenger silenced by personal reflections of human achievement.

On their last morning in Beirut, Johnny shrewdly negotiated a discount at Dave's hotel. As Eden looked on, he noted with some delight that this knack of doing deals was a typically Lebanese trait. Their ancestors, the Phoenicians, had been the world's greatest merchants and traders. The skill had stayed in the blood obviously.

It was this same charm and forthrightness that had contributed to the success Eden had enjoyed in his career, and he now felt he could see where that had come from.

'I have that gift of the gab, almost like a salesman, I guess, and that is something that is typically Lebanese, way back to the Phoenicians when Lebanon was the great spice centre of the Middle East. And it had always been a trade centre. Lebanon was a banking centre before it got bombed in the seventies. It was the one place where there was a lot of money – where the rules didn't apply. So it was full of salesmen who were articulate and smooth. Lebanese people generally are gregarious and easy with their words. And that is me, too.'

But they were also people of enormous generosity. Johnny had introduced the Gahas to his family and friends, to Beiruti nightlife and to so many other things. 'Lebanese people will have you into their home and give you the last morsel of food out of their mouth; give you the last drink of water out of their tap,' said Eden. 'It's just the way they are. They are always friendly and always welcoming.' Just as Eden had been told they were.

Eden, of course, insisted on paying Johnny at the end of their adventure together, but Johnny would not take any money from him. It had been no trouble; it had been his pleasure, he said, to have them in his Mercedes Benz.

At last they were on their way to Bechmezzine.

As they travelled up through the northern provinces

of Lebanon, they took a break in Byblos. It was, after all, impossible to merely pass by a city that had been continuously occupied for seven thousand years. Byblos is said to be the place where the Phoenicians invented the linear alphabet. It is a place where one can see the layers of time, the ruins and relics a reminder of all who had passed through there. As Eden and Nicola soaked up the Mediterranean sun, ambling across the glassy sea on a paddleboard, Eden looked back at the city and thought, 'Wow, this is in my blood. This is part of me. I come from this wonderful, ancient, surviving culture. To be one of the many faces in the crowd, too; to look like everyone else and to have people looking at Nicola, this blonde girl walking past, staring at her instead of me . . . It was like: I fit in. I was tall there, too, and I'm not a tall man, but I was the tallest person in Lebanon.'

Eden was now also more conscious than ever that the heart of this journey was yet to come: Bechmezzine was not far away. Soon Naseeb would be in his village. 'On a lot of other things he was approaching senility,' said Eden. 'But when you got him on his childhood and youth and the things that were really important to him, he was crystal clear. And what was really important to him, genuinely, was to see Bechmezzine before he died. It was his absolute priority. He knew exactly what he was talking about and he'd almost painted himself a mental picture of how it was going to be. One of my biggest concerns was that it would ultimately let him down. And then he had started to get really antsy on the way,' said Eden. 'All he wanted to do was be back in his village.'

This part of the journey was Ubbi's, and it was his grandson's responsibility to take him these last few steps of the way. It was Naseeb's moment in the Lebanese sun, and a time for Eden to reflect on all that had brought them there.

Eden had always known the theory: that migrants had come to Australia in search of a better life. 'They left behind everything they knew. They left behind their family, their friends, their relatives, their work, their language, their culture, everything, to travel halfway around the world to a country they never knew existed, in search of nothing more than a better life for their children, a better start for their kids, and in doing so, many of them, not all of them, I mean I think the Greeks and Italians were pretty good at hanging on to what they had, but certainly the Chinese and, to a degree, the Lebanese, in my case anyway, were pretty good at trying to assimilate. At saying, my kids need the best start. I'm going to make them Australian.'

He knew that as fact. But that skill at assimilation had meant the sum of all they had given up, and the journey they had taken perhaps lacked practical illustration or personalisation for Eden. Well, now, he was about to get the most personal illustration possible.

The morning before they travelled their final leg to Bechmezzine, Eden and Naseeb took a last walk through the stony ancient streets of Byblos. They passed men sitting on the pavement hunched over backgammon boards and stalls selling various souvenirs. Naseeb showed Eden the correct way to wear the fez, on a jaunty angle. They visited a shop selling musical instruments like the durbeki drum and stringed oud that made the sounds of Lebanon's tradition. Eden tried the small wind instruments on offer, laughing at his inability to get more than a single note out of them. The mood was light, but Eden could feel Naseeb's anxiety growing and his, in turn, with it.

They rounded a corner, passing beneath a graceful medieval archway, the old paving stones resonating with their footsteps and the countless footsteps of those who'd come before them. It was quiet and cool, and solemnity enveloped them. Eden asked Naseeb how he was feeling.

Naseeb shows Eden how to wear a fez — it's all in the angle

'Very excited. Very excited,' the old man said. And this time Eden knew better than to push for more. They walked in silence for a while, Eden with his hand clasped around his Ubbi's, until Naseeb, in a small voice offered, 'But I start to cry.'

Eden looked at his precious, frail grandfather, at his tears. Love and fear surged through him at once. Maybe he hadn't done the right thing bringing him here. 'Why?' was all Eden could ask, and Naseeb took some time before he could even attempt to explain.

'The music,' he finally said. 'The music made me very sad.'

Dave Kelly was behind the camera, watching this man of few words nail it yet again. The music; it made him sad. The music; it was the expression of a nation's soul. The years of longing that resided in Naseeb's own soul, yearnings for home, for family, for connection, the things he had happily suppressed for the sake of his new life in Australia, now unfurled at the sound. The music was calling him home.

Dave had to stop filming. He was too teary to see.

On the road from Byblos to Bechmezzine, Eden tried his best to distract Naseeb from his suspense. 'Our name was originally *Jeha*. When our family came to Australia they thought it was too hard for the English speaking people to get their tongue around, which is hilarious because they have more problems with Gaha than Jeha.

'Every time in Australia when I say my name is Gaha they go, "What?" They can't spell it. They go, "G-A, G-E, Galah . . . ?"' Eden said, hoping he'd get a response from his Ubbi with this one.

'They can't say J-E-H-A,' said Naseeb proudly, for he was in Lebanon now, where the name was not changed, nor pronounced incorrectly.

'But here,' Eden continued, 'I say to people my name is Eden *Je-ha* and they go, "Aaah, Jeha; I know the Jehas".'

'Don't say G-A-H-A,' said Naseeb. 'Say J-E-H-A. They know the name. They know the name Jeha.'

'Jeha,' Eden pronounced with his best Arabic flourish.

'That's right,' said Naseeb, genuinely thrilled at his grandson's interest in their name.

Eden's diversionary ploy had worked. Momentarily, anyway. Naseeb had something else altogether on his mind as they drove, something that was about to make Dave Kelly realise just how daring Naseeb could be.

Not far from Bechmezzine was the town of Kfar-Hazir. There lived Naseeb's first cousin, Rose Malouf. Naseeb had not seen Rose for seventy-five years. And now he was just going to drop in on her unannounced.

Daring indeed.

Seventy-five years . . . It had been that long since he first left Lebanon with his sister, Josephine. Such a journey. Naseeb was nineteen then.

As they drove into Kfar-Hazir, it all came flooding back to Naseeb, like a movie on fast forward. He remembered 1920, when France was given Mount

Lebanon by the League of Nations. Lebanon had not existed as a nation prior to this, but rather as a term, almost as old as the land's human history, to describe the mountainous region hugging the eastern rim of the Mediterranean. Even so, Naseeb's people were Lebanese. Always. They didn't need nationhood to tell them that.

As a child Naseeb saw how the French colonists pushed for the creation of a Lebanese nation against the wishes of the Arabic world but with the support of the Maronites, the Lebanese Christians. In 1926, the French and the Maronites drew up a constitution for power sharing between the Christians and the Muslims, heavily weighted to Christian dominance. It would plant the seed for Lebanon's future troubles.

The same year, Naseeb had left Lebanon, but not because of politics. He left because his mother, like the Gahas to come after her, was a seeker of happiness and fulfilment. She could not live life half-baked. Just as her great grandson Eden needed to come to Lebanon to find meaning in his own identity, she had needed to leave this country to stretch to the full extent of hers.

Naseeb's father had been a philanderer and his mother, Helene, a woman before her time, had tired of the situation and gone to America to seek her independence and to explore the world of opportunity there. Considering this was at the very beginning of the twentieth century, it was little wonder that Naseeb had pride in his family. His mother took the youngest, Selwa, with her because the baby needed to be with her mother, and the oldest, Jimmy, because he could work. The plan had been to send for the other three children – Naseeb, Josephine and Assad – once she was settled and set up in the United States. But the plan failed because the US immigration laws changed, preventing the family reunion.

So it was decided that Naseeb and Josephine, who were as close as peas in a pod, would go to Australia to live with an aunty in Sydney. Their brother, Assad, stayed in Lebanon for some years before following them to Australia. Naseeb and Josephine's passage was bought on a ship bound for Port Said in Egypt, at the Mediterranean mouth of the Suez Canal. There, they were to join their ship bound for Australia. Naseeb remembered how on the ship to Egypt he and Josephine were cheated out of their cabin and forced to sleep on deck by a purser who had taken a bribe from someone who thought they were more deserving of the sleeping quarters than a couple of teenagers. And he remembered the kindly captain who passed them on deck and put his big woollen coat over them in sympathy, not knowing that his own purser was responsible for their predicament. It had become a very distant memory. But now, driving through the streets of Kfar-Hazir, it all flooded back. It was as if he'd left yesterday.

Naseeb remembered how, once in Sydney, he and Josephine were accommodated by his mother's sister, Aunty Freda, in her grand palatial house overlooking Randwick Racecourse. Freda was the matriarch of the Sydney Lebanese community at that time, and her husband and his brother ran a successful warehouse business in Redfern, which supplied all the young men from Lebanon with goods to take hawking in the bush. The next step up for many of those men was to open a country store.

The time came for Naseeb and Josephine to follow this well-trodden path and they left to open a drapery shop in the bush near Tamworth. They were a hit in their tiny rural New South Wales community of Werris Creek. Lively, humorous, good-looking and smart, they would light up rooms with their presence. The business had been a success, but love, of course, eventually split Josephine and Naseeb. Josephine married and settled in Cowra where she opened her own shop. Naseeb married Margaret and set himself up as a designer of women's clothing, with a factory in Oxford Street, Sydney. It was a hugely successful business; Naseeb was renowned for the beautiful wedding dresses he made for many of the Lebanese ladies of Sydney.

Naseeb and Margaret settled in Coogee, and there by the beach in the safety of Australia, they enjoyed their lives. No invasions, no warring religions, no political turmoil. Life had just rolled on, until Naseeb now found himself at ninety-four, back in Lebanon with his grandson, walking up the driveway of his cousin Rose's home, thinking of what he might say to her after all these years.

Yes, it had been quite a journey, and it wasn't over yet.

'We'll knock on the door and see if anyone's home,' said Eden.

'Yes.' It was all Naseeb could say.

'Your heart must be pounding, because mine is,' Eden said as he cradled his Ubbi's elbow, helping the old man up the long driveway.

'My heart is going bom-bom-bom,' Naseeb said.

The knock at the door drew young faces, peering through the screen door at this stranger with his very strange entourage, cameraman and sound recordist in tow, a taxi in the drive.

'Madame Rose here?' Naseeb asked as a woman stepped into view. All his nervousness had given way to exhilaration now.

'Who are you?' the woman inquired softly and in some confusion, eyeing the people and the camera on her doorstep. Then she smiled at the old man, for it was clear by the way he had spoken Rose's name and his gentle demeanour, that he was kindly and obviously had some special reason for calling like this.

Naseeb replied, 'Tell her it's a young man to see her. No, tell her it's an old man.'

They were not waiting long in the huge main room of the house before Rose, a small but still strong and healthy woman, her black dress covered in an apron, emerged from a back room. At the sight of her, Naseeb could not contain himself and threw his arms up in joy.

'Rosa! Rosa!' he cried.

She moved towards him, her head cocked, squinting to gain a better look at this man, so familiar and yet . . .

'Rosa!' Naseeb laughed. 'What is my name?'

And a moment later she declared, 'Naseeb!' After

seventy-five years, it took her less than a minute to realise who he was.

They embraced, tears flowing, taking each other in.

Eden stood to the side watching, moved to the core. His tears were simply of the moment. A beautiful perfect moment in which he could watch the years peel away from the two people before him, offering him a snapshot of their youth. And their bond. And for that matter, his bond. For this was his family.

'My grandson,' Naseeb said, and Eden kissed his cousin Rose three times. The whole trip might have been worth just those kisses.

Reunited with Cousin Rosa

Naseeb's eyes feasted on his cousin. How joyous he felt.

For Naseeb, seventy-five years might have passed since that ship left for the Suez Canal, but he now knew he had never really left Lebanon behind. It travelled everywhere with him, in his heart. It would travel with him, he knew, to the grave. As he and Rose sat outside and chatted over cool drinks, Naseeb was aware this might be the last time he would see her, but through her he now understood the nature of his connection to Lebanon. Despite seventy-five years, despite him being an Australian now, his connection to Lebanon had not diminished. It would not die. It was integral to his soul. He would go to a Lebanese corner of heaven perhaps. A Lebanese–Australian corner.

'You know,' Naseeb said to Dave Kelly as they got back into the taxi at the conclusion of their visit, 'she looks still the same. I mean, to look at her, you know, she was a good-lookin' woman.'

Dave laughed. Naseeb needed to hear Dave laugh. Without that, he might cry. Naseeb's mouth turned down solemnly and his gaze set somewhere far away, perhaps to a place where he and Rose would meet again.

There was essentially nothing about Bechmezzine to recommend it to a visitor to Lebanon. It was just one of many small villages clustered in the Koura province in the north of Lebanon. It was nearer the eastern coast than it was to the Mount Lebanon range to the west, but it was not a seaside town, therefore not a resort town. It was only a few kilometres from Lebanon's second-largest city, Tripoli, and though it still produced things traditionally typical to the area – olives, grapes and eggs – these days it acted more like a suburb, a place the office workers of the city came home to.

But there was much to recommend it to Naseeb. He remembered living in Bechmezzine when it was a beautiful place full of orchards bearing figs and quince. He remembered it as always sunny, in the way of pleasant dreams. And he had felt blessed to live there. He'd gone to school there, a very fine school that taught students Arabic, French and English, and that had nourished his inquiring mind as a boy. He had grown up there, loved and surrounded by his cousins and aunties and uncles, and his Bechmezzini friends. He had loved his time there, and though the circumstances of his leaving had been those of family turmoil and harsh economics, just as he remembered this village as always sunny, his memories shone with the good times.

Knowing this, Eden was mortified when they finally drove into the town. Bechmezzine was on the road travelling north to Tripoli, and trucks and cars zoomed through accordingly. Huge, new-looking houses had sprouted, overshadowing more traditional dwellings and structures. There was paving and concrete everywhere. Eden couldn't see one fig tree on that main road.

'I was concerned that what Bechmezzine had become would ultimately destroy him,' Eden said. 'I was really worried. I was thinking then, would it not have been best to leave it as a wonderful memory rather than to have taken him back and dragged it all out and shown him that it was not as he remembered it?'

Naseeb looked out the window of the car in astonishment. 'I don't know any of these houses,' he said. 'We'd better stop and ask for directions.'

Eden's heart had sunk to an all-time low.

Their taxi pulled up next to a middle-aged woman, her dark hair and strong-boned features not unlike those of his aunties. Naseeb asked her for directions to the home of the relative with whom they were hoping to stay, Naseeb's nephew Bchoura.

Leaning on the wound down window of the car, the woman inquired what Naseeb wanted with Bchoura. When Naseeb explained, the woman stepped back, wide-eyed and happily surprised. She clapped her hands together in amazement and reached into the car for Naseeb, who clasped her hand as she kissed him three times.

'So you know each other?' Eden asked.

'I am his relative,' the woman declared proudly, in English. 'He is my third cousin.'

So she was a Gaha. Eden joined in the family discussion as best he could. It didn't matter that his Arabic was virtually non-existent. There was an electricity in the air. The place was charged with Gaha belonging. Like Naseeb, Eden was now very excited.

The woman gave them the directions they needed. But she had already pointed the way. For Eden, he knew the way was forward on a path to connection. For Naseeb, it was back, to reconnection. And either direction was just fine.

They were expected in Bechmezzine. 'It was overwhelming,' said Eden. 'The way they embraced us as one of theirs; one of theirs come from the new world. They loved us like they had known us all their lives. There was never the Anglo distance that I was used to, the politeness. That went out the window. It was just raw, real and loving. And the people who recognised Ubbi when they first saw him and took him in and loved him like they were his own grandchildren, that made it wonderful for him. Once he was there, I guess it was in the water or the soil, he just clicked into this mode where he felt as if he had lived there forever.'

From the moment he arrived, Naseeb's conversation was full of questions about family and friends from the village. His nephew Bchoura, who knew many of the people Naseeb spoke of, was able to fill in gaps of his past companions' life journeys. As Naseeb had expected, many of those journeys had ended, but he listened intently and relished the stories, until the weight of nearly thirty years of catching up, thirty years in which most of his peers had passed on, became too much for him. He broke down and wept.

They were tears of sadness, but also tears of relief and joy: at last, he was in Bechmezzine. And they were tears

An emotional moment as Naseeb revisits his childhood home

of farewell: Naseeb knew this was the last time he would see his village.

A visit to Naseeb's childhood home was next on the itinerary and this, too, would be a confronting reconnection with the past for him. Eden helped his grandfather up the steep incline of the narrow winding street that led to the old stone house. As they approached, they could see that the house was unoccupied, and though to Eden it didn't appear in too bad a condition, to Naseeb, who remembered what it once looked like, it was dilapidated. 'God bless the poor old thing,' he said in Arabic as he poked his cane through the rotting wooden gate. To see his home so rundown made him sad. He led Eden through the gate and up the steps to the building.

'The gate's just fallen down,' Eden said, looking back down the stairs in dismay as the gate fell off its hinges.

'Let it fall,' Naseeb said, impatient to be inside. 'Let it fall.'

Upstairs Naseeb stepped into the room where he was born; Eden threw open the green shutters to let light fall on the cream stone walls.

'It's hard to imagine Ubbi as a child,' Eden said, 'and overwhelming to stand in the room where he was born.' This tangible connection with the past made real the fact that part of Eden had been born in this room; these origins of his Ubbi were his, too.

But for Naseeb, as he looked around the room, coming back to this place represented the end of a cycle. He knew his time was coming soon. Soon, he would be joining the departed Bechmezzinis.

Before Naseeb left his childhood home he tapped on the next door neighbour's door with his cane. To his astonishment his old neighbour, Bashir, was still living there. 'Bashir's little head popped out the window,' laughed Eden, 'but he took about ten minutes before he finally came out. He was this little old man and his clothes were sort of worn and torn, but you could tell he spent the ten minutes putting a hat, tie and jacket on. He came out

dressed like that, and he and my grandfather had a conversation on the street. My grandfather's neighbour from
when he was a teenager, still living there. I don't know
what the hell they said to each other, but they had a little
chat and then they went along their way.

'The hilarious thing was, Ubbi said, "Oh, this place
has changed so much. I don't know anybody in this place
any more." But every time we hit the stop button on the
camera, he'd run into someone who'd go, "Ah, we've
heard about you. We knew you were coming." He knew
everybody. And everybody knew him. He was a
celebrity. It was like the circus had come to town and he
was the ringleader.'

The ringleader was going to visit his cousin Helene that
afternoon, a one-hundred-year-old Bechmezzini woman
with kind sparkling eyes and wisdom in her smile. She
hadn't seen Naseeb in twenty-five years and had never
met Eden before, but when they arrived her eyes filled
with tears and she embraced them.

'A lot of what was said between Helene and Ubbi was
in Arabic so we didn't know what she was saying,' said
Eden. 'But it was so emotional between them, we got the
gist, that the two of them were just so happy to see each
other. She didn't speak English until her son, Roger, asked
her "What's the most beautiful word in the English language?" and she said, "Love. With love there is no quarrel.
We just have to love each other and be good to each other."

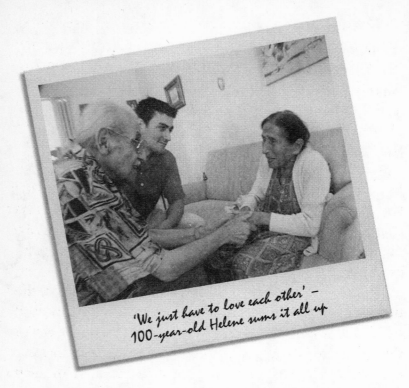

'We just have to love each other' –
100-year-old Helene sums it all up

'I was so touched. It was incredible, this member of our family who was an English translator during World War One and who had never really left her village, who hadn't spoken English for probably thirty or forty years, but who spoke with clarity when she finally got the opportunity. And who basically embraced everything about what had just walked in the room; you know, a man she hadn't seen for twenty-five years, his grandson whom she'd never met, and a camera crew.

'I mean, for someone my age that would be hard enough to get your head around, thinking what is going on here?

'I've grown up in a generation where we're searching for the meaning of life. We ask what life is, what's going on, why we're living this way. I guess the whole motivation for this trip was those kinds of questions.

'So what was really poignant for me in meeting Helene was I'd come all this way around the world and she was providing the answers.

'The simplest answers in life are the hardest ones to find. Sometimes you've got to travel halfway around the world to get them, and it just dawned on me: I had travelled all this way to hear, just love each other, just be good to each other, don't quarrel with each other and everything will be okay.

'And it was a true moment of clarity. Amongst all the turmoil, amongst all the reasons we'd done it, the turmoil of getting there, the financial struggle, finally we get to the village and the oldest person I will probably ever meet in my life answers something profound, yet with such wonderful simplicity.

'We were witnesses to a meeting between two old people who would never see each other again. She died not long after. It was one of those moments that would never be repeated. And that made it more powerful. I realised that had I not gone there at that time, I may never have experienced it.'

Leaving Bechmezzine didn't sadden Naseeb, it strengthened him. Having returned to the place where he had come into the world, his soul was made ready for its journey beyond this life.

But that journey would have to wait a while yet. There was some dancing to do in Beirut.

The evening before they left Lebanon, Uncle Edmund played the durbeki and Naseeb danced with Aunty Lilly and Nicola around the living room. Naseeb danced like a young man. He danced without a care for where his cane was. He shimmied and bent his knees and made Aunty Lilly laugh. He was celebrating. Completion. Victory. Achievement. The trip had brought all three. And so had his life.

It is said that the old often hang on for the opportunity to tell their story, or to see someone or their homeland once more, and then pass away soon after.

Eden found the truth in this.

Naseeb came back from Lebanon with a new lease on life. 'He was acting like a sixty-year-old again,' laughed Eden. 'And he started being a bit cocky and doing things he shouldn't have been as a ninety-four-year-old man, like walking without his cane, wearing his Cuban heels again. *I've been to Lebanon, I can take on the world. I can do anything.* That's just the kind of man that he was.'

Naseeb took two falls and ended up in bed, unable to move. It was time to leave. He developed pneumonia, which put him in hospital, and there he had a stroke. Five days later, he passed away.

Naseeb's legacy was enormous, for everyone in his family. They loved him deeply and he had loved them deeply in return. That people should just love one another and care for one another: no one knew that better than Naseeb – except maybe his cousin Helene.

His legacy to Eden was a world of beautiful memories: those nights of being spoiled rotten, watching *Sale of the Century* together, scrumptious meals of kibbeh, and the journey of a lifetime. Above all, in giving so gene-rously of himself on their trip to Lebanon, Naseeb had given Eden the gift of his own true identity. The gift of Eden's self.

'I no longer feel like an impostor,' Eden said.

He used to meet Lebanese cab drivers or Lebanese shopkeepers and they would ask him, 'Are you Lebanese?'

'Yes, I'm Lebanese,' he would respond.

The next question would be: 'Why don't you speak Arabic?' And the cycle of embarrassment would kick in again.

'They'd look at you as either a deprived child, or as if it was your fault. There was always this sense of guilt,' said Eden. 'Now, I seek out Lebanese people. I try out my bad Arabic on them. I can get in a cab and speak to a Lebanese cab driver with a few Arabic words. I want to go back to Lebanon because I loved it so much and I enjoyed the experience and because I want to look into my grandmother's side of things in the mountains and see more relatives on her side. And also continue to see other parts of the landscape and the country because it is endearing and beautiful.'

Eden had a point of reference now, some measure of his once mysterious heritage.

'I feel more comfortable as an Australian knowing about Lebanon, funnily enough. I understand how being an Australian is about being them *and* us. And I'm comfortable with the duality of being Australian. It's made me a better Australian; more understanding of the kinds of different cultures that go towards making up what it is to be Australian.

'But I also embrace everything about Lebanon. You look at the history and look at what the Lebanese have achieved over history, look at what's gone on in that country, on that soil, that's something to be proud of. And I'd never felt that pride until I got there, a genuine, sort of choking pride. And I thought I'd never feel that.'

And that song of the soul of Lebanon that had moved his Ubbi to tears in Byblos, moved Eden now. It called to him in a way he had never understood before.

'Arabic music gets into my soul now. Before I went to Lebanon, it was, don't have that playing too loud at the traffic lights. People might laugh at you. Now I realise it's in my blood. It's in my DNA. I can't deny it. It's silly to.

'It makes me feel more complete.'

Eden often recalls the sight of his Ubbi dancing. Dancing without his cane. Dancing with the exuberance of a Lebanese man, and with all the joy of his Lebanese–Australian life. The energy in this vision has made Eden feel like dancing himself. And sometimes, he does.

Eden, Nicola (back row, left), Naseeb, Aunt Lilly and Uncle Edmund (front row, right), with cousin Peshora Gaha and family

In his trip to Lebanon, as with all worthwhile journeys, Eden Gaha got more than he bargained for. In addition to a new sense of himself, he found a sense of fraternity.

'The wonderful thing about delving into issues of identity and ethnicity was that I realised I was not alone,' he said. 'There were a lot of people like me and a lot of people in the public eye who had fought their way to get where they were in their career against feelings of confusion over who they were; who felt the same way about identity as I did. So many people, I discovered, had questions – questions that couldn't be answered without a trip back.'

Inspired by that knowledge, Eden had become obsessed with the idea of making a series of documentaries along the lines of his own. He would accompany other Australians of different origins on journeys back to the lands of their ancestors, taking parents or grandparents with them.

He began hawking his idea, using his Lebanon documentary as a pilot. So powerful was the completed film and the concept he had created for a series that Eden received a Centenary of Federation grant, a broadcast deal with Foxtel's History Channel and sponsorship support from STA Travel.

Eden, Nicola and Dave were ready to ride again.

There was a long list of suitable candidates for the series, but narrowing it down to the required five was remarkably easy. Eden believed it all came down to destiny.

'The choices came to us,' said Eden. 'When we approached certain people and they started asking questions of: "How much will I be paid?" and saying, "I only fly first class," and that sort of thing, we knew that they weren't ready to do it for the reasons we needed them to. Whereas others thought, "I'll do this because it's important for me and my family." These were people who had a responsibility to family. These people didn't get paid. Nobody got a cent for spilling their guts. They flew economy class and stayed in three-star hotels, all of them. They did it for the right reasons.'

The first such person to come to them was Mary Coustas. The second film in The Ties That Bind series would follow the young Greek–Australian, her mother and brother back to Greece.

The roots of education are bitter, but the fruit is sweet.

ARISTOTLE

Mary Coustas
Greek Australian

Greece

Bitter Root,
Sweet Fruit

*'Friends who've gone back said something clicked for
them . . . There was a point of clarity. There was a point
at which the way you looked at life was going to be altered.'*

Effie had a mind of her own, a forceful and organic
invention that her creator, Mary Coustas, had not just
long accepted, but relished. When Mary donned Effie's
voluminous curls and Eurotrash outfits and stepped
into Effie's high heels, Mary was taken where Effie
wanted her to go. And Effie wanted to go all the way
to the top. Since the late eighties, when Mary first
wrote and played Effie, a mouthy suburban hairdresser
with virginal morals and hussy attitude, Effie had risen
and risen to become the Greek goddess of Australian
entertainment, taking her place alongside Barry

Humphries' Dame Edna and Paul Hogan's Mick Dundee.

Yet there were some places even Effie could not get Mary to go. Despite Effie's perpetual boasting of her Greekness, and Mary being one of the most recognisable faces of Greek Australia, Mary had not stepped an adult foot in Greece. In fact, she had studiously avoided doing so. It was enough to make Effie exclaim in her endearingly malapropos fashion, 'Oh my God! How embarrassment!'

Of course, plenty of first-generation Greek–Australians have never been to their homeland. At least Mary had travelled to Greece when she was seven. But what made Mary's non-appearance as an adult in the land of her forebears so 'embarrassment' was the weight of her contribution to the Greek–Australian landscape. She was the female embodiment of what it meant to be successful, popular, young and Greek in Australia. Her male counterpart in comedy, Nick Giannopoulos, was notorious for disappearing to Greece every year for a big chunk of the northern summer and Australian winter. Everyone assumed Mary did similarly.

Mary and Nick are two of the three Greek–Australian actors who have arguably done more for Australian ethnic relations with their works of comedy than decades of politicians could with policy and diplomacy. Mary, Nick and the third wheel, George Kapiniaris, had turned the Australian use of the word 'wog' into an affirmation of identity, claiming it for those against whom it had so often been bitterly used. They had done this through their groundbreaking stage shows, *Wogs Out of Work* and *Wogarama*, and their television sitcom, *Acropolis Now*. The shows took ethnic stereotypes, played them up, sent them up and shoved them up the noses of political correctness and racism alike.

Out of those shows had come Mary's larger-than-life Greek girl, Effie, and no sooner had she been introduced to the mainstream, than Australia was worshipping in the temple of her boofy hairdo. Australians loved that Effie wore her heart, sexuality and ego constantly on the fringed, sequined sleeves of her outlandish suburban disco get-ups. And out of Effie's glossy, candy pink-painted mouth came cracks, spoonerisms and not just a few words of wisdom that struck intergenerational chords. All this and she was a wog, a walking 'Greeks do it better' bumper sticker whose pride in her Greekness gave many a skip (or Anglo or whatever Effie chose to call an Australian of the pasty-faced variety) a severe case of ethnicity envy, and everyone of darker complexion a way to laugh at themselves and the treatment they might have endured in white-dominated schoolyards. Effie made it hip to be Hellenic. Hip to be a wog.

Against that background, it seemed mighty strange to Eden Gaha that his old friend Mary Coustas had not been to Greece for over twenty-five years. Here she was, expressing her Greekness in her art, embracing it for all the world to see, yet her homeland was largely a mystery to her. When Eden approached her about doing a trip to Greece for *The Ties That Bind* documentary, he discovered that it wasn't simply a case of Mary Coustas just never getting around to going to Greece because of the nonstop action of her career. He found that she had clearly defined reasons for avoiding Greece. But he also discovered that perhaps his timing was perfect. It was kismet. After years of keeping away from Greece, Mary's mind was turning back there to find out who her people were.

Mary's reasons for not going had been incredibly strong; they had arisen from the death of her father in 1987. Her beloved dad, Steve Coustas, died of a heart attack after a long struggle against heart disease. He was only fifty-nine. His daughter was just twenty-three. It hit her hard. Mary and Steve had been extremely close, and his death was not only a profound loss for Mary, but it became a source of incredible pain.

From the moment he came to Australia in the 1950s to the year of his death, Steve had been under enormous pressure. In addition to the challenges of making a new home, learning a new language and new customs, like many migrants Steve worked long and hard not only to support his nuclear family in Australia, but also his relatives in Greece.

Steve had his first heart attack at the tender age of thirty-three, revealing the presence of a terrible, incurable heart disease the year before Mary was born.

'Those people back home in the Greek villages, some of them thought that money grew on trees in Australia,' said Mary. 'They felt left behind and they saw the future as so much rosier in Australia. They didn't really appreciate the level of stress that a lot of the migrants were under to assimilate, to work, to raise their children. And they put a lot of pressure on the relatives in Australia to send money back.'

Mary's father worked eighteen-hour days, providing for his children's tertiary education, for a middle-class family life of which they could be proud. Steve also sent a cheque back to Greece once a month, and extra cheques for special requirements. He was a Greek man and Greek men had their pride. They needed to be seen to be able to provide for family. They also had strong loyalty to their people. It was in their blood. Steve could not turn his back on his family in Greece any more than he could have turned his back on Mary.

When Steve's sister had needed money for her dowry, he had provided it. Back then, a woman in Greece stood no chance of marrying unless she could provide the *prika*, the collection of goods and money offered to the in-laws to take the daughter off the family's hands. The demanding of *prika* was made illegal in 1983, but Steve's sister had reached marrying age before that time. Steve also paid for her wedding.

'He kept giving and giving and giving,' said Mary. 'But he was so fantastic about the way he did it that I suppose people would have thought it wasn't a problem. That's because he was bigger than that. He didn't want to make anyone feel guilty about the fact that he was under a lot of stress. He was the kind of guy who would have helped out if he could have and he did.

'But migrants like him, they just got so much pressure to make money that it was devastating to a lot of families and took the carefreeness out of life for the first ten or fifteen years in Australia. They all worked really, really hard and my dad was just one of them. He worked way too hard – obviously.'

And then he died.

In the years after his death, Mary was haunted by feelings that Steve's efforts had gone unappreciated and unrecognised by certain people back in Greece, the same people who had put pressure on him for money. Even in his passing, she felt that these relatives did not give due acknowledgement of his contribution to their lives. She feared going back to Greece because she did not know how she would react to seeing those people.

She might have become the big success, the role model Greek–Australian woman. Her alter ego might have been Effie, the Greek goddess. But not so deep down, Mary Coustas remained a little Greek–Australian girl who had lost her dad, and missed him very, very much.

Fourteen years after Steve's passing she had not stopped missing him, but something inside her had been gradually softening. Though she had been avoiding going back to Greece, she knew her path would eventually lead her there. It had always been leading there. It was just leading her the long way; and along the way she would create a new set of experiences she could own and command. Steve had always been her barometer, the person she measured all things by. She needed to become her own measure.

'I had learned so much from his life that in order to divorce myself from the sadness of the loss, I had to create some distance and relief from this big important thing,' said Mary. 'And the fourteen years since his death had been about that; about creating my own life.'

Finally, Mary felt she had gone down that path far enough to be able to go back to Greece and revisit the early part of Steve's life without feeling overwhelmed by her emotions. 'Time is a great healer,' she said. 'And time gives you distance to divorce yourself emotionally a little bit more.'

Time also meant that as clearly defined as her reasons for not going to Greece had been, the reasons *to* go had now gathered strength and lucidity. Her circle of friends included a number of first-generation children of migrants, many of whom had been back to their motherlands. 'Friends who've gone back said something clicked for them,' Mary said. 'There was a point of clarity. There was a point at which the way you looked at life was going to be altered by what you saw or what you heard or what you felt.' Mary wanted to test that theory for herself.

But there were yearnings that came directly from within herself, as natural and renewing as the turning of the seasons. Mary was looking forward to the next phase in her life, as a wife and mother. She knew, as well as she knew her love for her father, that she wanted to be those things. But to be them, she felt she needed to put to bed those big, terrible resentments of her twenties; the resentments she carried as a result of the death of her father. She knew that to honour the kind of parent he was, to *be* the kind of parent he was – unbegrudging, giving – she had to free herself.

And then, of course, there was her mother: her beautiful, funny, strong mum, Theophani, or Fani, as she's known to her family and friends. Fani was very much alive, and very keen for her daughter to go back to Greece. While Fani went back regularly on her own, she longed to travel to Greece with her daughter and son.

'It was my dream,' said Fani. 'I always dreamed of taking my kids to Greece, to my village, to my people.'

So, by the time Eden approached Mary about the trip, it was impossible for her to say no. With a little parental emotional blackmail from Fani, a growing willingness on Mary's part, and all the mutual love and respect that characterised their relationship, mother and daughter accepted Eden's offer, and Con would join them.

'Having my mum say it was a dream for her to have her son and daughter in her homeland with her was also a really nice way of saying to me, "This is something you need to do",' said Mary with a smile. 'But instead of making it sound like she was telling me what to do, she said it was something that meant a lot to her and she knew how important she was to me. So she was clever in the way she got what she wanted. And what it boiled down to was the fact that all she wanted more than anything was children who were happy.'

And Mary knew Fani was right: this was something she needed to do.

Mary had travelled everywhere but Greece before she finally stepped foot in Athens. 'It took a lot to get me there,' she said. 'Going back to Greece was going to bring up a lot of stuff for me. So I just kept avoiding it. I'd go to Africa, New Guinea, anywhere else.'

As if to prove the point beyond doubt, even then Mary managed to delay her arrival just that little bit longer. Fani arrived in the Greek capital with her son Con, accompanied by Eden and his wife Nicola, cameraman Dave Kelly and his wife the photographer Joanna Kelly, but with no Mary. When Mary had decided she was finally going to Greece, she had also decided to take in a big chunk of the Northern Hemisphere – while she was in the neighbourhood and all. On the way to Greece, Mary stopped off at Los Angeles, Boston, New York, London, Ireland and the South of France for the Cannes Film Festival. She'd taken the long way again. Or perhaps the final length of the long way.

But when she at last passed through Greek customs and pushed her luggage trolley through the final doorway between her and Greece, she kissed hello the mother she had not seen for three months, took a deep breath and then quipped, 'I've been to London, I've been to Ireland, I've been to paradise but I've never been to me – and that's why I'm here.'

She was always going to say something like that. Mary had long given up denying she used comedy to deal with pain. It's often the way of funny people. She was no different and there was no shame in it. Humour had seen her family through some terrible times. 'I probably learned from watching my dad and my mother do that,' she said. 'Every time there was something dramatic happening, it was also always an opportunity to defuse the drama by focusing on the bizarre.'

And so, there in the arrivals lounge of Athens airport, with Dave Kelly's camera rolling, she made a joke. She had just got there. She had not settled in to the emotional terrain. She could hardly say she was nervous and worried and scared. A joke would suffice.

Mary was in Athens, a city she did not remember much of from her trip as a seven-year-old, but a city she did not expect to like too much this time. She had visited the glamorous capitals of America, Britain and the South of France over the last few months and she did not imagine Athens would compare favourably. The airport concourse gauntlet of touts for taxis and accommodation, the madness of the traffic on the way to their hotel, the smog, the plethoric ugliness of the new fighting viciously with the beauty of the old, all seemed to confirm her expectations. These images were hardly the stuff of the Greek tourist brochure: the whitewashed streetscapes and brightly coloured boats bobbing on jewelled water. Athens did, however, have plenty to show for itself to Mary: the ruins of the ancients, the seething cultural clamour of layers of history in the seven-thousand-year-old seat of civilisation, the opportunity to hear Greek speakers all around, see Greek faces like hers in the majority, knowing this was the capital of the place from which her family had come. But she remained reserved.

Leaning on her balcony railing looking out over the city below and the Acropolis dominating the horizon, all she saw was unfinished business, a screen of uncertainty that obscured her view. She realised then that all those years of creating that life for herself had layered on top of the disappointment she felt at some of her father's relatives, smothering but not extinguishing it. Here, with her life stripped back, she gave air to that pain, Greek air, and it rose up, as large as it ever was, demanding her attention.

Mary and Con take stock at the Acropolis

But that afternoon, as Mary walked around the city with the others, the power of the Acropolis snuck up on her. No matter where you go in Athens, it watches over you. And no matter how hot or dirty or crowded the city gets, no matter the strength of the personal demons you are wrestling, an accidental glimpse of the ancient structure tends to put things in perspective. A majestic embodiment of the wonders of the past, of wisdom and innovation and spirit, it filled Mary with thoughts of her father's strengths and gifts. Steve could sneak up on Mary still, too, and quiet her soul just as powerfully. She began to feel then that Greece was welcoming her and that she was welcoming it into her being, knowing very much that she was doing what her dad wanted her to do. 'He was proud we were following in his footsteps,' Mary said.

Mary and Eden, Fani, Con, Nicola, Joanna and Dave passed through shady cobbled side streets where shops selling icons abounded, among them pictures of the Virgin Mary complete with tiny glowing red globes. The shops nestled snugly next to small cafés, their tables spilling out across the street, filled with Athenians drinking *caf*, the iced instant coffee drink favoured locally. The blue glass evil eye watched from everywhere, behind counters, in front of counters, over doorways, on doors, around necks, and followed the Coustases and their companions up the hill to the big marble sentinel that watched over all the blue glass eyes: the Acropolis.

'That's the rush you want,' Mary said as they reached the summit of the hill at the centre of the city and stood in the shadows of the long columns of the Parthenon.

Mary wandered off a bit on her own, then stood silent and still, feeling again her father's presence and approval. One thing Steve Coustas had instilled in his children was a sense of there being no time like the present. He had been acutely aware of the tenuous nature of tomorrow. If Mary hadn't been there yesterday, then she knew her father was glad she was there now. Now. There was nothing else.

The probability of sudden death had given Steve Coustas his heightened awareness of the present and it was an awareness that had shaped the lives of his wife and children also. The idea that Steve might leave them at any moment was simply part of their landscape, and had been since Steve had his first heart attack. From then on, the spectre of death was always present at birthdays and weddings. It was at name days and Christmas and Easter. It was at breakfast, lunch and dinner, in sleeping and waking, and in every breath each one of them took. But Steve and his family refused to be cowed by their intimacy with death, instead they chose to live with it, and live to the fullest for as long as Steve was with them.

'I like to laugh as much as everybody and I do a lot of it every day,' Mary said. 'But I look at life as a pretty serious prospect. Everything is important as far as I am concerned, that's why everything deserves appreciation and attention. No point in saving it until it's too late. That's the thing that possible death before I was born taught me. No point in delaying. You say it, you feel it now; you don't do it retrospectively. That's no use to anyone. You celebrate at the time. You do your best. You try to learn. You try to evolve. You try to help. You appreciate. You be thankful.'

Well, finally Mary was living the truth of doing now, feeling now, not delaying, and as she stood there in the symbolic heart of the Greek state, she was thankful she had come. She was learning, evolving and appreciating. And this was just the beginning of her trip.

As powerful as the Acropolis was, she could not help but look forward and beyond it. It was not a marble heart she was seeking there in Greece. It was the living heart that pumped with the blood of her own that she sought, and that could only be found in her relatives, in their villages up in the north of the country. Now that she was in Greece, she was anxious to get to them, and to get to the core of herself. But there was one more experience waiting for her in Athens, one which would bring her closer to that core.

'The majority of the things that impress me lie in emotions and experiences and in people,' said Mary. 'That's what I'm into. I mean, a tree's not going to come to your funeral and a house isn't going to be able to tell you anything. Every day of my life is about people. And if I go to great places, I have to consciously make an effort to take photos and to notice. You know, I love great art direction. Don't get me wrong. I love a nice street. I love a nice house. I like nice things, but they're secondary to character.'

That first night in Athens, amid the bustle of the

markets, the glitz of the nightclubs, the grandeur of its ruins, Mary found her focus on character. She, Fani and Con had arranged to meet Alex, a relative from Steve's side of the family, not someone towards whom Mary felt any of that resentment, but a man seeking only to reconnect with family. When he joined them for a drink after dinner, Mary was overwhelmed by how quickly she felt a connection to him, an empathetic blood love. He was a man who long ago, when he was very young, had lost both his parents in a car accident. He was raised by grandparents who had now also passed away. And in his company Mary began to feel the pull of the ties that bind, a gentle tug waking her sense of extended family from a fourteen-year slumber.

'I'd lost my dad. That was it. But that man who came to have a drink with us, he had lost everyone in his life,' said Mary. 'He was so alone. He didn't want to leave us at the end of the night. He walked us to the hotel and it was so . . . I mean, family is everything. To know that you've got someone there who looks like you, who sounds like you. Family is everything.'

In that meeting Mary understood a little better the reasons why her dad could never say no to requests for money. Family was everything, and when Steve and Fani left Greece for the first time, it was that 'everything' that they could not leave behind.

Mary had a photograph of Fani as a young woman taken the day she left her village in Greece for Australia. The black and white snapshot was small but the moment it captured was enormous and multi-hued, textural and kinetic. Fani's family – mother and brothers and sisters – were arranged around her. The expressions on their faces reflected a stoic acceptance that Theophani's leaving was what must happen and that sorrow would necessarily come with it. There was no attempt to hide distress but it was controlled. Neither was there any evidence of chins being forced up. There was an honest dignity in the acknowledgement of sorrow and also in the acknowledgement that Fani's leaving was an affirmation of possibility, of life, of moving forward.

Later, after the box brownie had been put away, the eighteen-year-old Theophani had clung to the two columns of the portico outside her mother's house, crying 'No, no, no', even though it had been her decision to go to Australia.

'She got cold feet at that last minute, not because she didn't want to go, but because she was about to go to the other side of the world, away from the people who had been her world,' said Mary. And though the grief would give way to the excitement of new possibility, Theophani would always miss her family back in Greece.

'I always asked my mum, at least once a year, are you glad you made that decision to come to Australia?' said Mary. 'Her response varied, depending on what was happening in her life. Usually, ninety-five per cent of the time, she said yes. But at times after my dad died, when she didn't have a support structure under her, when she had to mourn without her mother and her sisters, when she couldn't be a daughter, be a sister, the response was different.'

It was true. Forty-five years after leaving her village that first time, Theophani still felt the emotion of the event like it was yesterday. But only sometimes. She loved her life in Australia. And if she missed Greece too much, these days she just went back.

The two days Mary spent in Athens exceeded her meagre expectations.

'It was a lot more modern than I thought it would be,' she said. 'I just got this feeling that Athens was a hole, because it was literally in one, but I didn't expect it to be as cultured or as European in that groovy way as it was. So I was really pleased to go out and see how beautiful the restaurants were and how the lifestyle had become so modern European. The Greeks, I think, are primarily known for their character and their history and not for the way they live their modern lives. So it was really good to see.'

More than the intrinsic charms of Athens, it was the connection with her father's relative on that first night that had opened her eyes and set her stomach aflutter, excited at thoughts of discovery and healing. Not only had she enjoyed the city, but she had enjoyed her first encounter with extended family and it had put a piece of the jigsaw into place; a small one, but a crucial one nonetheless. They were all crucial to completion. It put her in an optimistic mood for the rest of their trip.

The next leg would take them to Thessaloniki, a city that could only have a positive effect on the psyche, with its bright coastal light and fresh salt air. Perched on the northernmost point of the Thermaic Gulf in Macedonia, Greece's second largest city is a sophisticated place of waterside promenades and colourful markets, youths on motor scooters and fashionable, expensive boutiques, tavernas and bistros, Byzantine churches and Roman ruins. It was also a city of Coustases, which is what interested Mary the most.

There's a Greek belief that life has a way of balancing itself out, sorrow and joy in equal proportions. Too much joy might invite enormous sorrow. So it was important to say a prayer to give thanks for great joy, to ward off the inevitable balancing dose of sadness. But for Mary, sadness might also have invited its equal measure of joy, because the sorrow she felt for Alex, her long-orphaned relative in Athens, as well as her own past feelings of disconnection, were about to be balanced sweetly in Thessaloniki.

In this city lived another Mary Coustas, of which Effie would be mightily proud. This Mary Coustas owned a bridal shop, a symphony of girly fantasy, of chandeliers and gilt-framed mirrors and parquetry floors, ladylike velvet-upholstered benches and enormous white dresses.

'This is Mary who plays Effie on television in Australia,' the other Mary Coustas proudly announced to her staff as she kissed and hugged her namesake. And Australian Mary laughed because she knew Effie meant little in Thessaloniki.

'I am glad that I was not known as an actress in Greece because sometimes that can get in the way of getting to know a person – if they are already impressed,' she said. 'They knew that I was an actress and that I had had a little bit of success in Australia. But that was it and that was great.'

Mary was still a star there, though, because she was a woman on her first adult trip to the homeland. And because of that, Greek family pride burst forth, frothing and bubbling with celebratory joy like the acres of white tulle that hung along the walls of the salon.

That afternoon, it was the women together, laughing, drinking coffee and eating sweet biscuits; crying and kissing and hugging and stroking each other's hair in unbridled affection. 'Anyone who knows Greek families knows that the women are the strongest in the families most of the time,' said Mary. 'They might take a supposedly subservient position, but they are the spines of the family.' There, in that bridal shop, the Greek women were loud and loving, free and individual, and they laughed till they ached.

Mary felt part of something bigger. For so long, the tight-knit unit of her immediate family had been her world. Her father and mother were her sky, the earth she walked on, the air she breathed. They had given meaning to her existence. And now, here was another layer to her existence, a parallel universe where she had existed in people's thoughts and prayers, and where people knew her because she had resided in their hearts, and in their family pride and love. Mary opened up to their warmth like a flower.

Fani had to cross herself with a prayer of hope that so much laughter would not balance out with the same amount of tears, especially now they were on their way to her village at last. She prayed for happiness there. God had answered her prayers to get her children this far – back to Greece. Perhaps He was listening and would answer this prayer, too: that the joy they shared in Thessaloniki would follow them for the long-awaited reunion in her village.

It was a long, long drive from Thessaloniki to Florina, which lies right near the border where Greece meets the former Yugoslavian republic of Macedonia, not far from the tri-country point where Albania joins the picture. There is not a lot about the area to make it a feature in guidebooks, other than its gateway function for rail and car travel and its lively markets that bring together the eclectic wares of the surrounding countries. But it is not far from what is believed to be the site of Mieza, where the great philosopher Aristotle is thought to have taught, and it is not far from Nympheo, the birthplace of the great philosopher in Mary Coustas' life, the young Greek man called Stergios Coustas, otherwise known as Steve, her dad. Slightly further north is Mesokambos, the very last village on the road before Yugoslavia, and that is the village in which Theophani grew up. In the guidebook of Mary's life, Florina and its surrounds were to be an absolute highlight.

The drive, however, was a little less comfortable than it might have been, on account of Mary's luggage. Eden was astonished at how one small woman could have so many big bags. Mary protested that she'd been travelling now for three months. She'd accumulated stuff. Plus she had scripts, her computer and books with her, not to mention hair products and makeup. She and Eden bantered about it for all the joke was worth – anything to help divert their attention from the fact that, thanks to all that baggage, they were crammed in like sardines.

In the long miles across the vast agricultural plain that stretched northwest of Thessaloniki, through fields of peach trees and grapevines, conversation turned to what was ahead. Outside the car, though, it seemed as if time were doubling back upon itself because the scenery of long ago was the scenery of the present. This area was off the tourist trail and out of the way of change. If anything, change moved in reverse here; the land appeared to be settling back into itself, as it had in many rural regions throughout Greece, where village life was in decline, village populations dwindling as cities continued to grow.

Fani settled back into herself, too. Watching the miles roll by, she felt the years roll back as she and Mary talked about the history that had brought them to this part of Greece now.

Up the mountains and along a nauseatingly winding road from Florina lay Nympheo, a wealthy village by Greek standards, Fani explained, especially compared to her own village of Mesokambos. Mesokambos had been ravaged by the exodus of the young people who had left Greek village life for cities or who had gone along the path blazed by her generation, the path towards new lives in Australia or Canada or America. Nympheo, on the other hand, thrived on its beauty and lush greenness. The differences between Mesokambos and Nympheo clearly illustrated the extremes in the Greek landscape. Mesokambos was arid, flat, dusty and sparse, its buildings utilitarian. Nympheo had always had the cool, dewy verdancy that concrete-bound city Greeks dreamed of on oven-hot summer days. Just as in the days when Stergios Coustas was a boy, Nympheo cradled a collection of bluestone and earth-coloured mud-brick houses, inns, coffee shops and churches. Horses galloped in nearby paddocks or clip-clopped on cobbled streets. It was against this backdrop that Stergios grew up; in startling contrast to the village life Theophani knew, yet so close by. But fate would wait until they were both a world away from here before drawing them together.

After completing his obligatory military service in the Greek army, young Steve had set about exploring what was on offer in his immediate surrounds and then in Thessaloniki. But opportunity and his own adventurous spirit beckoned him to explore far beyond the life he had known. He had heard how Australia, this young, sunny country full of possibilities, was welcoming migrants. And so, just as Theophani had gone to Australia and become Fani, Stergios went to Australia and became Steve.

One fine Sunday in the late 1950s, Melbourne's growing Greek community was taking its *volta,* its social stroll, in the grand inner-city Exhibition Gardens, meandering among the flower beds and stately European trees, pausing to sit on park benches and watch the world go by. Two years after her arrival in Australia, Fani was there with friends, strolling, chatting, sitting, sunning. On that Sunday, Fani saw a man she had never seen in the Exhibition Gardens before but whom she instantly recognised from elsewhere. He was a man she had seen on a bus one day. On a bus back in Florina. When she saw him that first time on that bus, she thought he was the most handsome man she had ever seen. They didn't speak. That was that. She got off the bus. She went to Australia.

Steve and Fani's wedding

But now, here he was, that handsome man again, in this park, in the middle of inner-city Melbourne.

He was Steve Coustas – and mutual friends had already decided that Fani and Steve, both single, would make a good couple. They were introduced, fell in love and married soon after.

The world was experiencing the post-World War Two boom and Australia along with it. The country needed labour and so had opened its gates to European immigrants. Steve had believed the brochures. He thought Australia was going to be a good place to be, this place where you were invited to come and set up a life. He didn't expect to be walking into the top job at the pointy end of town, but he did think he would be presented with the opportunities of which he had been told, and he was raring to take them, no matter how challenging. He never imagined that he'd ever be a small cog in a long assembly line, but that was how Steve Coustas found himself – a small cog on the assembly line at the Astor electrical goods factory.

Steve Coustas was never one to accept unsatisfactory situations, though. He was always one to meet life and its challenges with the same passion and drive that took him away from Greece. And so he thought to himself, 'I didn't leave my family, my village for this. There's got to be more. There's got to be another way.'

So he left the assembly line – with no other job to go to, and few prospects.

'That was quite radical because, like most of them who migrated then, he came over in debt,' said Mary proudly.

'Not only did they not have money but they had borrowed to come across. So they had to pay off the debt, they had a responsibility to pay back their family, they had to find their feet, they didn't know the language . . . I mean, it was just obstacle after obstacle after obstacle.'

But Steve Coustas was also never one to be defeated by obstacles, no matter how wide, how high. He always found a way around them. It was simply in his nature to embrace life and regret nothing. He opened a restaurant in Gertrude Street, Fitzroy. It was called The Five Fs after the Greek words *filous fere filous, fae fige,* which translates as 'friends bring friends, eat and leave'. It was a successful restaurant, but unfortunately the partnership behind it was not, and the business failed.

Unbroken and undeterred, Steve Coustas turned to the trade he had learned in Greece and set himself up as a house painter. Before long he had a thriving concern.

'You have to understand, my dad was an unusual sort of character,' said Mary. 'He was a bit of a superstar. He was so liked that opportunities opened and my dad was smart and moved on those opportunities and created a good business for himself. He worked an enormous amount of hours.'

Mary remembered how her father's passion for life fuelled his success, ensuring that the Coustases became the first family in their neighbourhood to get a car, first to get a washing machine, first to get a television, first to go back to Greece.

First to do everything, the Coustases were also the first of the Greeks to move out of Collingwood. Mary was nine when the family made the move from the then industrial inner city to the Australian-dream outer suburbs, as many Greeks and Italians, seeking better lives and bigger backyards, eventually would.

'Right, that's it,' Steve had said before the move. 'We've achieved what we set out to. My children are going to end up with less options if we stay here so we bite the bullet and we go somewhere middle class to give them access to better schools and we see what happens.'

'And he was right,' said Mary. 'As much as I fought it. The last thing I wanted to do was move to Doncaster when Collingwood was my home and there were people that I knew there. I loved that whole village feel of having all those different cultures and all those doors open and action on the street and people sitting on lounges on the veranda talking to you as you walked past. But he was right. And he was always like, "Yes, my life could end in the next six minutes or the next six months but life goes on and let's make these moves now".'

The new house in Doncaster was a typical, outer suburban brick home on a quiet suburban court. But the backyard was magnificent, all tree ferns and wisteria vines, and a big barbecue constantly put to use. 'That's why we bought it,' smiled Mary. Fani, preparing dishes in her beloved kitchen, Steve out in the backyard with the barbie, the dog and the kids, Mary dancing around him, treating him like her big doll, making fun of him. A Coustas family Saturday afternoon.

They were happy days, mostly. The only sad days were when Steve suffered a heart attack. And he had a few of them. More than a few. One year he had more than one a month. And Fani, who might have been sleeping next to him or sitting on the sofa beside him watching television, would save his life, many, many times.

Steve's illness did not quell his spirit, though; and he never allowed it to quell the spirit of his family, even when he was very ill or housebound.

'There were days when he couldn't leave the house because of a smog alert or because he was on twenty pills a day and it affected many different things,' said Mary. 'So we'd open the doors and he would walk continuously in a circle from the kitchen, through the family room, down the hallway, through the lounge room, and around again. So you'd be watching television and about every twenty seconds you'd get him walking by, between you and the screen. That was how he did his exercise in the house.

'My dad would be lying on the couch and he'd say, "What are you doing? What are you up to tonight?" I'd say, "Oh, I'm going to go out," or whatever, and he'd make some crack. And I'd put the blanket on top of his head and walk out of the room. I would have a shower or talk on the phone, put my makeup on, come back and the blanket would still be there. I'd pull it off and he'd go, "Jesus, I thought you'd never come back".'

Or Mary might find him standing at the sink attempting fancy cocktail-maker moves with glasses. 'You'd walk over and there'd be five broken glasses around him and he'd say, "What do you want me to do? I can't leave the bloody house".'

Fani cried with laughter at Mary's reminiscences, as they continued their drive towards Florina. Bouncing off her mother's delight, Mary now recalled the time when Steve, during one of his housebound periods, called an extraordinary family meeting in which he unveiled a new schedule for them, built around the notion of no radio or television. 'At seven o'clock we're having breakfast,' he'd said. 'Whoever's cooked does not wash. Whoever doesn't wash at breakfast, does so on the lunchtime shift. From nine until eleven-thirty we go off and do what needs to get done. At eleven-thirty we're back, preparing for lunch which we have at twelve. Again from one till three we have two hours off to do what gets done. Three o'clock, back here: compulsory laughing for half an hour.'

'Well, the next day was the first – and only – day we started this routine,' said Mary, 'because at three o'clock we're sitting there, all of us who have never known a day in our lives not spending some time together, we're just looking at each other going, this is so ridiculous: compulsory laughing. And then there's this pause; nothing's happening. And then he just starts with this stupid laugh and keeps pushing it and pushing it till we all start laughing because it's such a ridiculous thing, not only as a laugh, but as an exercise. We did it for one day and that was it. But he knew we weren't going to do it again. He was just so much fun. He was full of life, you know.

'So alive and so current all the time, like he'd say, "Have you heard that bloody song on the radio?" And you'd go, "Which one?" And he'd go, " 'It's America'. Oh bloody hell, I'm sick of that, everything's about America." And I'd go, "Dad, the song is, 'It's a Miracle'."

'"Ah Jesus, Mare," he'd go. "When are you going to wake up to yourself? Everything's about bloody America." He was just hilarious.'

Even his serious side was inspirational for Mary. A great thinker, he would choose philosophy over discipline. 'Don't look at the obvious,' he'd say to his children time and time again. Every day of Mary's life with him she remembered him saying, 'You've got a great brain. Use it.'

He questioned why, at eighteen, she didn't yet have a boyfriend. 'You're too bloody picky. That's your problem,' he'd said to the daughter he adored. 'Just go and get yourself a boyfriend. You don't have to marry him. Just go be young.'

'He was always profound; extremely. And my dad was very grateful and maximised everything and taught me to maximise everything,' said Mary, even though Fani was always on at her to ease off a bit.

'Mare, you do too much. You need to slow down,' Fani said now, though she knew she was wasting her breath. She saw Steve's work ethic in her brilliant daughter and, while that might have been cause for concern, she also saw his unstoppable passion.

'I might be a workoholic and I do work a lot,' conceded Mary. 'But I still see my friends every night. I have been programmed to know that any minute someone might go. If the phone rings, there is always the thought in my mind: has something happened?

'He taught me that life is now and you've just got to get in there and make every move you can make and get the life you want for yourself. Don't expect anything from anyone.'

Mary had long ago taken her father's advice to heart, and that advice was in no small way responsible for Mary's own success. 'You need to write,' Steve had said to her. 'That's what you do really well and that's how you're going to control your destiny. You've got to create. You can't expect other people to stop living their lives to open doors for you.'

Nor to keep them open for you. Melbourne's St Vincent's Hospital had dubbed their regularly returning patient 'the man who should have died'. The emergency and cardio staff had seen Steve, time and time again, stand on the precipice of death and hover there, only to turn around and trudge the steep, perilous path back to life. Once back, he did not let the trip weary him, but greeted life with reborn enthusiasm. He was with those he loved and he owed it to them to love them with as much vigour as he could. And as Mary remembered his tenacity in life, her thoughts turned naturally to how they had ultimately lost him.

On a day in 1987, he went to the edge again. He had one extremely severe attack. 'And he should have died then,' said Mary. But again he resisted. Two hours later he had another heart attack. The doctors kept him alive for a couple more hours. They were holding the door open. Steve lived as he preached. He closed that door, and passed away.

Mary remembered the silence of the moment. It was that moment in which the souls of the living fully understood and celebrated the flight of the soul of the dead. It was a strangely beautiful moment. 'The silence, you know exactly what death is then, and you just think, why undermine it with sound?'

But the sound of grief soon followed. 'A lot of it. Just gutteral sounds that you didn't want to hear, sounds that were as emotional as you were going to get.'

Three days after Steve Coustas' death, Mary's career took off. She was on stage and touring with *Wogs Out of Work*, the show was receiving rave reviews and setting box office records. As advised by her father, she had begun to open her own doors, having hooked up with fellow performers, Nick Giannopoulos and George Kapiniaris, to forge that success.

'Yeah, I think he got upstairs and started pulling some strings quick smart,' said Mary. 'He planted a lot of things in my mind about the type of career he thought I could have . . . he thought that I had the power to create my own destiny. He thought that I should write and produce material for myself, to not wait for someone else to see what I was capable of, and to have some control over my own future. He was very entrepreneurial like that. He encouraged that.'

Looking back on that time, Mary could see now that, because of her touring, she wasn't around her mother as much as she might have been in the terrible early grieving period. But as their genetic map had been written, the Coustases just had to do what the Coustases had to do. In Mary's case, that was following the destiny Steve had always said was hers. For Fani, that was going into mourning, donning traditional black, despite Steve's express wishes. 'Don't wear black. I'll come and haunt you,' he'd said. Nevertheless she wore it for eight years.

'I don't believe in black, but while I was very, very upset, any colour you put on me at that time I could never accept it,' said Fani. 'I didn't think I was going to wear it for eight years; maybe three, four, five. But I couldn't wear colour.'

'She was unapologetically mourning him twenty-four hours a day,' said Mary. 'She wasn't going to pretend everything was all right. She turned inwards into the couch and bawled her eyes out for three or four years. But I said to my brother, "She's got to do what she's got to do. Whatever gives her peace of mind".'

'But,' said Mary, 'she wouldn't die. She wouldn't die. No way.'

'No, I want to live,' laughed Fani.

The Greeks are a very superstitious people. In death, they believe, there are dangers for the living. If the dead come to you in your dreams and ask you to go with them anywhere, even if they just ask you to cross a room because they want to show you something, you must not go. You must say to them, 'I'm fine here, thanks.' If you go with them, you will die in your sleep. Steve came to Fani in her dreams. She didn't go with him. She turned to him, there in the place between living and dying, and said, 'I'm sorry, but I didn't send you there early. No way am I coming with you. I'm living for my kids now.'

Despite her sadness, Fani was a Coustas. She knew they had one life each and they had to live it as best as they could. For Fani that ultimately meant focusing her energy on her children. And for the family Steve had nurtured to have such faith in the future, that meant treating his passing as more than just a monumentally sad event, but as an auspicious start to a new phase in their lives. Mary's instant success after his death seemed proof of it.

'The worst thing that could have happened at the time did. We survived it. There is something that we will always miss, but sometimes an incredible change comes about. I mean, my mother's way of handling it was amazing. My mother was reborn, I mean totally reborn after the mourning process,' said Mary.

For a while there had been a running joke at the Coustas house about this new Fani. If the phone rang and one of her children was there, before she answered she would mutter wryly, 'Very popular. Yes, very popular.' It cracked all of them up. But it was true. Since Steve's death, Fani Coustas had become very popular. She'd even done some acting herself, appearing in television commercials. She learned how to drive. She got involved in community activities and became the president of her social club. 'People were just open mouthed,' said Mary. Fani also began travelling back to Greece for two or three months every year.

With the death of Steve came freedom of movement; the freedom they did not have when he was alive, because they always had to be near a hospital. Not that they ever, ever regretted or begrudged the circumstances of living with him. He was their superstar. But following his death, they did their best to embrace the positive possibilities of their new situation. It couldn't take his place, but it gave his death some meaning. And life new meaning.

That freedom meant there was nothing standing in the way of the fulfilment of Fani's dream: to go back to Greece with her adult children. Nothing standing in the way but Mary's reticence. Until now.

Going to Greece was always going to stir deep feelings for Mary. Her history with her father had included many stories about his young life in Greece. He would love to tell her stories about where he grew up, about this place through which she was now travelling. Her mind was awash with vivid images, movies made in her imaginings of her young father in the land of the great philosophers, poets and almighty gods. They excited her. But for so long that excitement had been overwhelmed by feelings of loss and resentment for those she felt had not acknowledged his importance.

Mary's brother Con had been back before. 'My brother had always been far more spiritual than I. He saw things in a much bigger way,' said Mary. 'He said of those relatives, "Well, that's the way they are and they've got to live with that and that's that." But I had felt for many years that I had had to fight being incensed on the inside. And I had felt like someone had to say to those who did not appreciate my father, "You don't know what you had. He was the most exciting person in the world and you didn't even know that about him. You were just interested in how much money he had and whether he could send you more in order for you to live your life to the fullest".'

The residue of that anger still sat uncomfortably in Mary's heart, but in a few hours' time everything would change.

Mary, Eden, Con, Fani, Nicola, Joanna and Dave piled out of the car to stretch their legs at Edessa, a tiny town perched on an escarpment overlooking vast, seemingly unending flats of crops. From the mountains above, streams trickled towards the Katarraktes, the waterfall spilling a long silvery cascade through deep cool green to the fields and orchards below. Edessa was only an hour away from Florina, and as they strolled along the banks of streams that meandered through shady parks, Fani recalled this place from her childhood. She looked at her children and simply could not believe that they were here with her now. God had been listening. This was a heaven-sent trip.

Eden asked Fani how she was feeling at that moment. 'I'm feeling nervous,' she said, fussing with her pearls like worry beads. 'And thinking about my people. After I lost my husband I always prayed: "God, please help me. One day I want to go to Greece with my kids".'

Fani couldn't finish. Tears welled up and choked off her words.

Mary and Con looked protectively to their mother.

Fani had been through so much with her own family as a wife and mother, and she had had to cope with it all far away from the family that cherished her as a daughter and sister. She had longed to bring those two realms of experience together. And now she was doing so. In a very positive sense, this was the end of her dream. But she had held that dream for so long, the thought of its imminent fulfilment was overwhelming.

Fani tells Eden of her dream of returning home with Mary and Con – it's about to come true . . .

Fani made her way to Edessa's tiny, icon-lined church to make a prayer and give thanks. She and Mary each lit a candle for Steve. And in their contemplation they both realised that, like drops of rain coursing towards the Katarraktes, they were each nearing a precipice, a moment of completion. For Mary, it would mean her reconnection with her mother's people. For Fani, her wish come true.

In that last hour heading into Florina, Mary recalled her visit to this place when she was seven years old – and how she'd flaunted her Western ways and wares.

'I was very fashion conscious. I remember wearing white Levi's and a yellow knitted top and talking to my cousins about fashion and saying, "In Australia we wear this and in Australia we do this and you know Suzi Quatro? That's the sort of hairstyle I've got." I remember going into town and acting like a big nob and trying to impress them with how inner-city Australia I was. They were pretty impressed. I think they thought I was an idiot, but they were pretty impressed.

'I remember my brother in my mother's village with a slingshot, aiming at the animals. In Melbourne, we lived on a main road. We didn't know that you had to respect nature because the chickens provided the eggs, the cows provided the milk. It was just, "Oh yeah, this is another thing to muck around with".'

One of Mary's most vivid memories was of her mother, this woman who had not seen her family for twenty years, 'doing the wife thing'. Steve, Fani, Mary and Con stopped to see members of Steve's family who were living in Florina and, though Fani was all the while consumed with the knowledge that her own family was twenty minutes away, Mary remembered her mother's control and quietness. And then her anxiety the next day as they all piled into a car and drove to Mesokambos. But more vivid still was the memory of arriving there: the whole village had come out to see Theophani. They lined the streets, from the school on the corner to the church on the next corner, around that corner to the next church on another corner, then around that corner and right down to the home of Fani's family.

'Now, my mother didn't even know what her younger brothers looked like because she'd left them as children. She wasn't sure that she'd recognise them. They had all those years of growth and maturity that she had missed out on,' Mary explained, remembering Fani's excitement that day as she stepped out of the car and into her village for the first time in twenty years. Then suddenly all Fani's nervous energy exploded and she was running down the road and the bystanders lined up were calling out their hellos, and Fani was crying. 'Her family obviously knew who she was because she was the mad woman running down the street overwhelmed and emotional,' said Mary. 'And she saw them, and the crying, oh my God, they cried for days. And days. We all cried. I mean, what words do you use for something like that? They just sat down and they cried.

'And so my brother and I, for the first week or two back in Australia, we were doing it like a comedy routine, sending it up, running down the hallway, acting out the scene. We laughed about it because it was so dramatic. We didn't know what else to do with it.'

On this trip, though, there was no one lining the streets when they finally arrived in Mesokambos. Indeed, they had all been so focused on Con's map-reading skills that the village had snuck up on them. This time, Mary, Fani and Con walked along the street to Fani's childhood home in silent anticipation. Walking up the road to her mother's house, Fani could barely utter, 'There is my brother,' before emotion silenced her and everyone there. The only other words, 'Welcome young people,' came from Fani's brother Pantali, who open-heartedly acknowledged Eden, Nicola, Joanna and Dave, before he was overcome, too.

The family comes together again

Mary, the woman who was a seven-year-old girl the last time she was seen in Mesokambos, was enfolded in family, one member after another, a wordless communion.

And then the small wizened woman in head-to-toe black who had been sitting on a wooden chair beneath the portico waiting, watching for the arrival, stood up and lifted her cane, taking her weight firmly without aid, so she could hug Mary with the power of all her ninety-odd years, her large, strong hands enveloping the grand-daughter she thought she might never see again. She stroked Mary's hair and kissed her face, and Mary Coustas was home.

No fear any more, no distance. She was there, right there with all her being.

For Mary, the manner in which her mother's family members related to each other was a revelation. She marvelled at it. She was so proud to come from people like these.

'Before getting there I thought that I'd be irritated by small-minded responses to things; by not being able to have the conversations that I'd delayed for so long, to not have acceptance and therefore not have the possible dialogue that you can have when someone accepts differences.'

But her fear could not have been further from the reality. Since the first night of feasting and throughout the second day of conversations held one-on-one with her relatives, Mary opened up fully to the notion that extended family had the potential to be a firm foundation for identity, greater than its potential to be burdensome. She had yet to meet her father's people, but meeting with her mother's first had created a place of peace within her, one from which she could perhaps not forgive the wrongs against her father, but at least put her own anger to rest.

'I'd been constantly told by my mum how good her side of the family is and I'd always been like, yeah right. I mean, my mum's slightly biased. But they were just walking hearts on legs. I could not get over just how beautiful the males in the family were. I remember the females from '72 as being really welcoming and loving. But the boys, my cousins, really blew me away. They didn't take anything the wrong way. Their sense of humour was really to my way. We had a lot to laugh about which was fantastic. They were just beautiful. They were overwhelmingly beautiful. My spirit was singing from the moment I got to the village.'

A few days into their stay, while boating on the deep sapphire blue water of the Prespa Lakes, Mary stretched in the sun and took a deep dose of the fresh, clean air of her people's land; she felt at home, serene as the lake itself, as she looked back at her experiences and impressions of Mesokambos.

There had been no enormous epiphanies, no earth-shattering revelations, no soul searching or heart wrenching. It had simply been about family. Playing with little cousins, drinking Nescafé frappe, the iced coffee, with big cousins, holding the hand of Sonia, her grand-mother, and noticing, with amazement and delight, that some of her own physicality, the way she talked with her hands, the way she held her head when she listened, were her grandmother's, too. She had not seen her since she was seven, and yet they shared these things. These were things that meant much to Mary.

Mary cherished the simple moments, like sitting down to dinner and having her uncle seated next to her, rubbing her back affectionately. 'When he was in Australia he got used to me, he was around me a lot when I was a kid. And so we had a connection. Also, his English was still really good. So when I hit a wall with my Greek, I was able to put my thoughts into English and he translated,' said Mary.

'One night I was falling asleep in my cousin's restaurant, just trying to stay awake listening to the guys talk without their parents there, and what struck me as the most beautiful thing was that my mother's side of the family was very warm, very affectionate towards one another and they showed a lot of respect in that sort of extended family way. The boys were really considerate and hard working and there was not a lot of that macho Greek thing that I found a little bit too much to handle . . . the guys were very affectionate towards one another and I thought that was beautiful. They didn't have that "Oh, don't worry about us, we're just the losers you left behind" thing. They were really keen to know what we were doing and to know what kind of lifestyles we had. And they talked about their lifestyles in a way that was full of pride. I was thrilled.'

Mary was also thrilled to see her mother with her people. 'I thought she'd drop into this sort of bland person in the village and play a more traditional role. But she did that for about five or ten minutes, then flipped back into her own character. She was so addicted to the liberated way she lived her life that she sort of infected the village with that.'

Another special memory, another simple moment occurred on a drive to Florina. 'I was in the back seat with my mum and my aunty, and my brother was in the front with my cousin Con, so the two Cons were in the front and we were just singing and laughing all the way and I just remember thinking, look out of the car and see where you are because you need to give this context. And it was all rolling green hills and I just thought, stay in this moment but remember this feeling, because it was what I hoped would happen. It was this feeling of being yourself and looking around the car and seeing fragments of yourself physically in others. I didn't have many relatives in Australia that were first cousins or whatever. Most of them were in Greece. So it was really gratifying being able to see parts of me in other people.

'My biggest fear for many years was that there would be written on my epitaph, "Here lies a good kid." I thought that would be the ultimate martyr thing to have as the final words written about you. And when I see my mother's side of the family and they're all so fantastic, so giving – they're not rich, there's no doubt about it – but they would give you the last mouthful of food, the last cent they had, the last bit of energy before they blacked out from tiredness. That pleased me. I no longer felt like I was out there on my own with my want to please all the time. I now felt like that was coming from some-where real. They were all good kids.'

After their stay in Mesokambos, they headed for Corfu, the main Ionian island off the west coast of Greece, where the Coustases could relax, just be tourists for a little while, and take in all the island had to offer: its softer light, the emerald greens, the smell of the Cyprus trees, the French-inspired streetscapes of Kerkya. They laughed and enjoyed the sunshine, and Mary told happy stories of being with her dad.

As a child at Greek name day celebrations, which would always bring several families and many friends together, Mary Coustas would play in the backyard with all the other kids, but come dinnertime Steve Coustas would make sure his beautiful daughter entered the room with him. It didn't matter if everyone in the room knew Mary, as he entered he would always call the entire gathering to attention. 'Ladies and gentlemen,' he'd say. 'I'd like to make an announcement. I'd like to introduce my daughter, Mary.'

'Oh, Dad!' Mary would protest in the sing-song whine only kids could muster, 'they all know me already.'

'I know,' Steve would whisper back. 'But I'm proud of my daughter. I want to introduce her. What's wrong with that?'

There was nothing wrong with that. Despite com-plaining to her dad, Mary loved that he loved her so much, this charismatic man whose presence was made all the more magical by the precariousness of his life. She relished each and every moment she had with him.

'He was the best toy,' she said. 'He'd let you do anything to him.' Like the dreadful haircuts she gave him. Walking down the street behind him shortly after one such episode, she recalled whispering to her mother, '"Oh Jesus, look at his hair." There were bits missing. Holes everywhere. It was just so random, you could see his skull. And my dad, he was walking up ahead and he turns around and goes, "What are you laughing at? Are you laughing at my haircut? I know it's not a good one, but my daughter gave it to me".'

Fani guffawed at Mary's retelling of the tale, and Mary's eyes shone with the memory.

On Corfu, there was less of the anticipation of those early days in Athens and Thessaloniki. For Fani, the return home had been everything she hoped it would be, and for Mary, it had been a clarification of notions and feelings that had milled around her forever in undefined colours and shapes, coming together now to create a perfectly lucid picture of who her people were and how she fitted in with them. Who she was. It had given her great strength, and prepared her for the journey still to come.

After their couple of days on Corfu, they would be returning to Florina and heading up the mountains to Nympheo where they would see her father's people.

But already, the acrimony that she had long anticipated would overpower her upon meeting Steve's family had dissipated. She was far more confident now of what her reaction would be when she met her father's relatives, and she was looking forward to seeing most of them. The enrichment she felt at getting to know her mother's people had whet her appetite for more. She knew now there was no point in confronting anyone about past wrongs. It would only hurt everyone. Besides, her father had always been a proponent of live and let live. He would want her to remember that.

Mary recalled coming home one evening, having had a disagreement with a friend. She had expressed her frustration at her friend's opinions, to which Steve had said, 'But that's the way they look at the world. You're not going to change that. Why do you feel you have to? Just accept that this is what they're like and that's the experience they're bringing to your life.'

She remembered, too, how Steve had explained to her why he wasn't angry about his illness: as in everything he did, Steve took responsibility for it, owned it. At a time when he had felt under enormous stress, Steve had gone into the backyard one day, looked up to God and said, 'I need some physical proof that I can't take this pressure any more. Give me a heart attack, something, show these people that I can't handle this, that I can't do this.' Six months later he had his first heart attack.

'He told me this two weeks before he died. That was important for me to hear because if I hadn't, I might have *really* been angry. I always just kept wondering if he was angry. I mean, one year he had thirteen heart attacks of varying degrees and he never got angry. You just expect people to get angry with their bodies disappointing them and limiting the life they can lead. But not my dad. He was just fine about it. He got bored with being a prisoner in his own body and he would do the most bizarre things and that's why he was so funny because he needed the release. But he never got angry.'

Mary could at last honour that part of his spirit by overcoming her own anger. By taking the high road, as forged by her dad.

They arrived in Nympheo on a Sunday. Sunday was a big day in Nympheo. Though many of Steve's old friends had left the village for Florina long ago, every Sunday they still travelled the forty-five minute, winding ascent to Nympheo. Up there, in the perfectly preserved village surrounded by beech forest, they gathered in a small café constructed of local stone and talked of the old days and the new. It was here that Fani found them and introduced her daughter. These were men who had known Steve well; one of them had even visited him at a time when he was very sick.

Mary kissed the people with memories of her father and stood back, watching her mother speak to them in Greek. She was thrilled to meet them. But she suddenly felt more acutely than at any other time during her journey the aching absence of her father. And yet somehow, equally as strongly, his presence. He was there in their memories, their knowledge of who she was, their exclamations of how much her brother and she looked

Fani, Con and Mary are welcomed by Steve's old friends in Florina

like Steve. Walking away up an overgrown path to see the house where Steve was born, Mary knew herself better than ever before.

'I don't really care about landscapes,' she said. 'I mean, the type of art I buy, or the photos I take, that's not really who I am. I'm a people person. And going to Nympheo, I saw a cross at the top of the mountain above the village and it was so beautiful. But it's the faces that stayed in my mind: the characters, the smiles, the words really stayed in my mind. Just going back and seeing his friends and having those kinds of conversations, just the thrill of watching people who knew him and loved him talk about him, that was such a gift.'

One of these men she would remember always. He was an eighty-year-old lawyer wearing a seersucker suit and a woven straw pork pie hat with a feather in it. They sat down with him for coffee. The old man could barely look at Con because he looked so much like Steve. He could barely mention Steve's name without sobbing. And he said to Mary, 'I feel so bad sometimes because I have lost siblings and I have mourned them, but . . . Just the person that he was. Just the person that he was. You know, there's not people like that out there any more. You should be elevated above everyone else just because he was your father. He was on another plane.'

If Mary's dad was not appreciated by some, just knowing there was an eighty-year-old lawyer in Greece who could not speak of her father without reverence was acknowledgement enough. Not that she needed to see this acknowledgement any more. Mary knew now that her appreciation and love were proof in themselves of her father's importance. She knew what she had. She understood it more than ever now.

When Mary finally met up with Steve's people in Florina, the anger was gone. Quite simply, she said, 'It all changed. I mean, ninety-five per cent of his family I adored and I got to meet all of them.' All of them except those few who refused to acknowledge the part that Steve had played in their lives; she had no desire to see them. 'It was like my dad said: they are what they are and you just have to accept that.'

That was how she reacted. She felt very proud and at peace. This was what Greece had given her.

Mary goes back to Greece regularly now. If she is in Europe, she cannot return to Australia without seeing her relatives in Greece.

'I know what I'm coming back to. There's no fear any more. I know I'm coming back to a place that makes me feel good. My family has made me feel like I was omitting a piece of the jigsaw puzzle before. Now it's in place.

'And I've got relationships with them that aren't about the family now. They know me and I know them as individuals now. It's also a bit harrowing, though, because if one of them is sick or something bad happens, you feel it a hundred times more. It's more attachments, it's more opportunities for highs and lows. And that's life.

'I think about them. I'm stopped at traffic and I think about what my grandmother is doing. That stuff wasn't an option for me before I went back. I'd be thinking about other things. I often think about myself in my grandmother, about how things skip a generation, about how I do things that my grandmother does that I haven't seen my mum do. And I think, wow, I got it from her and I'd only met her once as a kid.

'To see my mother's side of the family work the fields, just to see how the village works as a community, to see how Greece works as a country, just seeing everything about Greece, the people, my relatives, the place, the future, the philosophy, the way that they live – I feel much more at peace with being Greek.'

And in her relationship with her father: 'It has brought life and light to the memory. He'd be so happy to have seen my mother and my brother and me retracing his life and talking about him.'

Mary and her dad

There is a film in the Coustas family archives, of an early teens Mary, out there in the backyard at Doncaster, the barbie being prepared, the picnic table set. Mary was with her dad. Steve was bare-chested and the band of his boxer shorts was visible above his trousers. It was the seventies, and showing your undies was far from fashionable. Mary was trying to address the problem, attempting to tuck his underwear back down below his belt. Steve was laughingly maintaining his right to bare the band of his boxers.

It had been too painful for Mary to watch that film for many years after Steve's death. But she can watch it now. It still makes her cry, but the pain is less bitter; much more sweet.

Home is the sailor

Home from the sea

And the hunter

Home from the hill.

ROBERT LOUIS STEVENSON

Jay Laga'aia
Samoan Australian

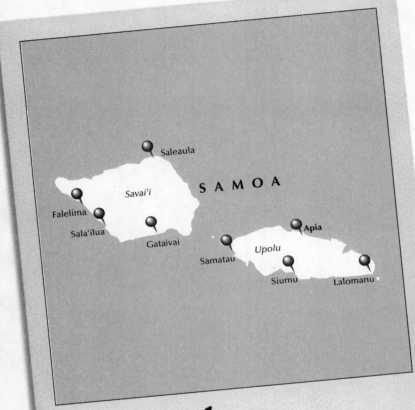

Samoa

Laga'aia
'Aiga

'I have long been aware of this chasm between doing what has to be done and being completely who you are . . . the things I had experienced at work, the circles I had moved in, when I stripped those all back, I didn't know if I would stand up as a Samoan. And as a person, really.'

Jay Laga'aia has the veneer of the consummate professional performer. A confident, handsome and charismatic guy who is also a proud Polynesian; that's what the world sees and it's a combination that has made him a solid living. His unique look, presence and talent have kept him in demand as an actor in the high profile TV shows *Xena, Warrior Princess* and *Water Rats*, and as an energetic and fun host on *Playschool* and *Surprise! Surprise!* He's also been cast in the blockbuster *Star Wars* movie *Attack of the Clones* and in the second *Lord of the Rings, The Two Towers*. Jay has also proved

131

himself to be very much the all rounder with his work as a stand-up comedian, musician and singer.

But appearances can be deceiving. Despite the spirited confidence that is Jay's trademark, and despite his success, there were times not so long ago when he felt he didn't measure up. It wasn't so much a case of feeling insecure about being a Polynesian man in a white world, but of measuring up to his blood history, as a Samoan man. He was concerned about the price he'd paid for success, what it had cost him in terms of his identity. He was known to describe himself as a 'coconut – brown on the outside and white on the inside', and it was meant as a joke, but he worried about the truth of it.

Jay's self-confidence was honed growing up in the working-class streets of New Zealand's South Auckland, the setting for the powerful film, *Once Were Warriors*. His heart, however, was Samoan. He'd been raised by staunch, proud Christian parents determined to keep the Samoan heritage alive in their children. It didn't matter that they lived in New Zealand; they were Samoan first. Jay and his brothers and sisters had been made to speak Samoan at home, taught to read from the Samoan Bible, told Samoan stories.

But for Jay, it seemed that everything he'd achieved had taken him further and further away from his origins. As a young man Jay had felt he needed to polish himself and take off the South Auckland rough edges to fulfil his dream of becoming a performer. And he did. But along with the rough edges, Jay felt he'd also sacrificed much of his Samoan identity in pursuit of a career in the white-dominated entertainment industry. He felt particularly the loss of language; the subtleties of understanding and communication.

Despite this, or perhaps because of it, Jay had always made a public point of his Samoan heritage. He knew very well that there weren't many Polynesians doing what he did, let alone Samoans, so he felt a responsibility to draw attention to it. 'Because I tread where a lot of Polynesians don't go, I feel I should always try to open the door for others to go through. I always feel that, yes, I will fly the flag as far as Polynesia and Samoa are concerned.'

In fact Jay's role as Senior Constable Tommy Tavita in the hugely successful Australian television series, *Water Rats*, was not originally written as a Polynesian until the series' creator Hal McElroy changed the rules. 'That was a Godsend,' said Jay, 'because Hal McElroy took this huge gamble to cast a Polynesian. It was a huge call. Originally, my character wasn't Polynesian but then they had this brainwave: "Well, hang on, we're sitting on the Pacific Rim. What would happen if . . ." It's much to Hal McElroy's credit. When I left *Water Rats*, I rang and thanked him. But mostly, they didn't write the big parts for ethnics. You had to keep proving yourself. I was always being put in my place as an outsider.'

Above every other success in his life, Jay had been fortunate enough to marry the love of his life, Sandie, who happened to be a white woman, not a Samoan. They were bringing up their three sons and their daughter in a white world, dividing their time between inner suburban Sydney and a middle-class seaside suburb of Auckland, while Jay's eldest son from a previous relationship was off studying in Japan.

When Eden Gaha approached him with the idea of taking Jay and his mother, Pofitu, back to Samoa, he thought it was a great idea, though he maintained he'd be doing it mostly for his mum. After all, she hadn't been back to Samoa for twenty-eight years and she wasn't getting any younger. Their first trip there together would mean gathering up family stories, and the documentary would stand as a lasting record for them and their family. It seemed like a fantastic opportunity; one too good to knock back – at least in theory.

As they began planning for the trip Jay joked about the standard of accommodation they'd look forward to. 'I mean, my idea of roughing it is a hotel with no room service. We're going camping? What hotel?' Jay knew all about hotels in Samoa because he'd been there once in 1990 to host a fundraising documentary after Cyclone 'Ofa devastated the nine islands of the nation. 'It was the first time I had been and I didn't have the benefit of going with any of my elders, my mother or my father. I turned up and they just thought I was a tourist. It was a huge shock for me.'

It had brought to the surface an issue that had really been a constant throughout his life: wherever he was, he always seemed to be an outsider.

'I look like a Samoan as far as I'm concerned. But over there I could have been Swedish. They were talking in Samoan as if I didn't understand and it was very confronting because if you are a Samoan in New

Zealand, Samoanness is beaten into you. And then I got to Samoa and there was no sense of belonging. In New Zealand I knew I wasn't a native. I was not Maori, so therefore I was one removed, even though I was born there. And then in my job as a performer on TV shows in Australia, they don't write for brown people and so you had to keep convincing people that you were good enough to do these roles.'

That meant Jay often felt he was putting on a façade so as to be acceptable in western society. 'Doing that, you just got further away from who you were. For example, I grew up in South Auckland and we spoke "street". But in order to be heard and be understood outside of those hardcore urban areas, I had to learn to speak English properly. Once I did that, people from the old neighbourhood would look at me and go, "You're a bit white, aren't you?" I have long been aware of this chasm between doing what has to be done and being completely who you are. Sometimes the person people see is not who you are. My fear in going to Samoa was: the things I had experienced at work, the circles I had moved in, when I stripped those all back, I didn't know if I would stand up as a Samoan. And as a person, really.'

This trip was also about the most important role of his life: that of family man. As it turned from an idea into a reality, Jay admitted that perhaps it wasn't just all about his mum. It was a little bit about him, too; about his search for identity and belonging, and his growing desire to measure up as a Samoan man.

'I'm always a Samoan. I can't deny that. But as far as

being in touch, I suppose I am not as much as I would like to be,' he said. 'As soon as I started having a family, having children, I realised it was imperative that I passed on what my father passed on to me: the stories, the culture. But it's difficult. Once you get far away from the proverbial tree, as I am now, because my father is long gone, it gets really hard to actually understand some of the stories because I can't qualify them with my dad. That's why this trip is so important. It is something that I will try and remember because there are stories there that need to be told.'

By the time the plans for the trip were set in motion, Jay's own reasons for going galvanised and so did his apprehension. Before the trip could go ahead he had to ask his mum, Pofitu, to go with him. For Jay, that seemed the most difficult part of all. A trip back to Samoa would be a deeply emotional journey for Pofitu. Could he ask her to expose that publicly in a documentary?

There was no doubt his mother was yearning to see Samoa again. 'She did say she had a fantasy about visiting. She said, "I would like to breathe the air again, to taste my history again".' If it was just the two of them, just family, Pofitu would go back there for a visit with him, but breaking the news to his mother, a very modest, dignified matriarch, that they'd be travelling with a film crew, and that she was to be one of the stars of the show, was another matter entirely.

'I once asked my mother, "Would you ever go back and live in Samoa?" She said, "No, the floors are too hard".' Jay laughed, knowing the truth in it. It has been said that Samoa is the last place where you can see the true South Pacific culture. That Samoa has been resilient to the changes that have swamped many of its neighbouring island nations might have been both a blessing and a curse for its people. On the one hand, Samoa has survived global homogenisation. On the other, many of its people still live in third-world conditions. Either way, many members of Jay's *'aiga*, his extended family, still lived the traditional village way in open-walled, thatched *fales*, sleeping on bedding on the floor.

Since leaving Samoa for New Zealand in the 1950s, Pofitu had dedicated herself to her six children and to her husband, Finauga Lavea Laga'aia, up until he died of cancer in 1983. After his father died, Jay had watched his mother struggle with her grief and slowly rebuild her life. Still parted from her *'aiga* in Samoa, she managed to pick up the pieces by drawing on her Christian faith and focusing her energy on her grandchildren. She still lived in South Auckland where she was a pivotal member of Samoan society and an active member of her church. And even though she missed Samoa she was sure she didn't want to live anywhere else but in New Zealand. Even when Jay went to Australia and took Australian citizenship, Pofitu opted to stay in Auckland. It was her home.

'She lives in New Zealand and travels to Australia to see us when we're there,' said Jay. 'I think she's content.

She has sixteen grandchildren. She has lived for them and her children since my father has been gone.'

In her quiet times, Jay knew that his mother longed for Samoa. But Pofitu didn't have too many quiet times. Between her church and community work, the comings and goings of her children and grandchildren, and her visits with them, there was little time for longing. When she was with her grandchildren, who played wildly as if they were in the leafy village plantation in Samoa instead of in the suburban backyards of Sydney, Melbourne or Auckland, she could stop one of them long enough to smell their hair and they would make her laugh, and then she did not miss Samoa.

'She says to me, "You are my island now. My family is my island. This is where I live now",' said Jay.

Pofitu always said: 'Jay doesn't know how to spell the word "scared". Since he was very young at school, he was always like that. He loved to sing in front of the whole class. All the other kids would push each other to move to the back. But Jay was always pushing to come forward and stand in the front line. That's how he is. He was never, ever shy and whatever he wanted to do, he just went and did it. He did it straight away. And I learned from him to never be scared of anybody. He talks straight. That's Jay. A straight talker.'

Well might Pofitu say Jay was scared of no one. Held up in Sydney filming *Surprise! Surprise!*, he waited until

Eden and Nicola Gaha were virtually on Pofitu's doorstep before asking her if she would go to Samoa with them. And when he asked her, it was by phone – so he could not get a clip across the ear, which no Samoan son is ever too big to receive from his mum.

Surprise, surprise, indeed.

'Jay rang and he said, "Mum, get ready. These people are coming. We must get ready to go to Samoa",' remembered Pofitu. 'I said, "Jay, are you out of your mind? Who are these people?" And he said, "Oh Mum, they are very good people. You will know that if you meet them." And I said, "I tell you the truth. Don't you bring them here. I'm not going." And Jay said, "Mum, they are coming already".' Pofitu's brown eyes sparkled as she recalled laughingly that this conversation occurred on a Tuesday, and Eden and Nicola were due to arrive on the Friday. 'I said to Jay, "Well, let me think about it." But the next day, the Wednesday, when I came home from the church, Eden rang. They were already in Auckland!' Pofitu's body shook with laughter. She wiped tears of hilarity from her eyes. 'And I asked some of my other children: "What do you think? How can I go with those strange people I have never met before? I have never seen before?" And my other kids said, "Tell Jay if anything happens to Mum he's going to get it from us".' Pofitu laughed some more. 'And so on that day of their arrival, in my heart I said, "Do I go and see them, or do I just go and do my own thing?" But I thought to myself, oh, it's too rude to not go and see them. So I thought I would just go and talk to them. I did that and finally I said,

"Oh well, I trust you all," because they were so young and so honest. They were really good people.'

And so Pofitu was going.

'When Mum agreed to the trip,' Jay said, 'the calls started coming from my brothers and sisters in Melbourne, from around the world saying, "If anything happens to Mum . . ." My sister Deborah who is second youngest but basically the matriarch, she goes, "If anything happens to Mum, I'm going to kill you." And I'm "Hey, hey, hey! No need to get ca-ca-mouthed with me! Nothing's going to happen!"

'And then I said to Eden, "If anything happens to my mother, I don't care if you bring that Lebanese mafia around; I will kill your ass twice".' Jay laughed heartily.

Jay, Matthew and Pofitu on the trip of a lifetime

At the last minute, Jay decided to take his son, Matthew, on the trip to Samoa. Matthew, the oldest of Jay and Sandie's kids, a clever and gregarious nine-year-old, seemed ready to experience a trip like this. In 1999 Matthew had stood up next to his dad at the Sydney Town Hall and received Australian citizenship with him. Jay wanted to do it as a token of thanks: 'I thought, well, I live and I work here and this country has given me such an opportunity to sink or swim and so far we're dog paddling really well, that I needed to physically and publicly say thank you. So Matthew and I, we got our citizenship together. It was a great day. Matthew was so excited. He said, "Do we get a medal?" I said, "You've got to do the deeds first." He said, "I'm lucky. I'm a New Zealander in New Zealand and an Australian in Australia".'

And soon Matthew would feel like a Samoan in Samoa, for now, these two Samoan–Kiwi–Australians were going back to their ancestral home.

Jay said before the trip, 'I would never take him if my mother wasn't coming. I will be there to make sure he doesn't run on the road or get eaten by a shark, and to see he goes to sleep at night. Other than that, I relinquish full parental control to her because this is an opportunity for him to see with her eyes where his people came from, where his grandmother came from, where his family came from. He can dial up information on Samoa on the Internet and go, "that's cool". He can get a coconut shell and go, "yeah, this is a coconut shell". But to hear and to see and to live it and for him to be able to ask questions of his grandmother while doing that is a great opportunity and I can't deny him that. He'll get there and he'll hold his grandmother's hand and she will introduce him to his great grand uncles and all his other cousins we don't know about. She will show him where my father's village is and where her village is and what it's like to walk everywhere and not worry about the fact that you're not wearing a label.'

He added, 'Though I don't know how he'll cope with that. But he's a performer in his own right, Matthew, because it is in our culture; that is, because all the stories are passed on orally, it's in our nature to be performers. You look to Polynesians, they are all performers as such. And I think it will be eye opening for him to see that, to see where his characteristics come from. And to sit and listen to a proper church service and just listen to people sing. But I don't know whether it will frighten him or whether he will want to learn more.

'My oldest son speaks fluent Japanese. He's at school in Japan. And now Matthew wants to learn Japanese as well. That's great because you get into industry now and they all speak Japanese and it's good to be able to speak the language, but then I think now, hang on, he doesn't even know how to speak Samoan. I worry about it.'

Such matters appeared to be far away from Matthew's mind, however. He listened intently as Jay primed him with stories of Samoan and family history. But for Matthew then, the biggest thrill was in anticipation of a holiday, no matter where it was. And of travelling with his dad, without his tribe of siblings, and with another very special person in his life. 'I just couldn't believe that Nana was going!' he said excitedly.

When the time came to leave for Samoa, Jay was still in the midst of filming and his schedule was changing constantly so he and Matthew stayed behind in Sydney while Pofitu flew from Auckland with Eden, Nicola, Joanna and Dave. Despite her earlier misgivings, it didn't matter that she was alone with them, because Pofitu was now just so excited to be going back to Samoa. It had been twenty-eight long years since she had seen her homeland.

'We were still in the air,' said Pofitu. 'It was just before we landed, but you could already feel the Samoan climate in your body, the warmth, the humidity. And I said to Eden, "Oh! We are here! I am in Samoa. Wow!" And then we landed and Eden was talking to me but I could hardly speak. I couldn't believe I was in Samoa, finally. I had often dreamed about going, made the beginnings of plans to go, but too many things, especially my kids, would end up preventing me from going. But when the moment finally came, when I was landing in Samoa, oh, you don't know how much I thanked God for that day.'

As Pofitu stepped off the plane onto the tarmac at Apia airport and a flight attendant put flowers around her neck, the air and the sunshine made her feel like a girl again. And when Eden said to her, 'Home, at last,' Pofitu cried out joyously: 'Yeah!' And she laughed.

Home at last – Pofitu with Matthew and the crew

They drove to Apia's Aggie Grey's Hotel, famed amongst travellers for the late Aggie's hospitality, a legacy that lives on, and for playing home to writers and artists. Pofitu's heart filled with gladness to see the lush green hills, the white sand, bright red roofs and brown faces everywhere. Smiling barefoot children played with their dogs along roadsides and village life ambled by on Samoan time. Pofitu sighed long and deep, letting herself slow down to move apace with it. It was surprisingly easy for her. She was home.

Despite the relaxed island atmosphere, Pofitu could not shake a certain sense of urgency, however. She could not wait for Jay to arrive to begin getting in touch with her family. With quiet, nervous excitement, she put on a strand of pearls, tidied her bun and set out for the home of her late sister's husband.

Eden held her hand as she crossed the soft lawn that stretched out before the house. But as she walked through the door, all nervousness was swept aside. Her niece, Pela, who was not expecting her, greeted her in amazement. 'Look how pretty she is!' Pela exclaimed. 'I thought I would never see her again!' And the two women giggled like the girls they were when Pela lived in Auckland, hug-wrestling on the sofa like teenagers, punching each other softly on the arm and holding each other in playful headlocks, laughing, rolling about.

Pofitu's brother-in-law, Mai, shuffled into the lounge, curious at the hubbub. Old and infirm, with cataracts clouding his vision, at first it seemed he did not recognise her. But when Pofitu said, 'Hi darling,' and hugged him, Mai could feel the familiarity in her embrace, the unmistakeable warmth of *'aiga*. Pofitu held him and wept.

She wept, for that familiarity reminded her of her sister and parents, long gone. She wished she could hug them, too. It reminded her that she was older also, seventy-two now. Holding this frail man who had lost his teeth and hair, his bulk and strength, she remembered that once he was proud and tall like her son Jay.

As the sun set on that first day, Pofitu wore *lava lava*, the Samoan sarong. She put a flower behind her ear and walked to the water's edge. She hoisted up her hem and waded into the ocean, dipping her hand in and letting the soft, warm water trickle through her fingers. She walked a little in the sea, and the flow of memories was as fluid as the water, lapping all around her, caressing her.

'It's a blessing from God to let me go to Samoa at this time in my life'

'I thought then, I did this all the time when I lived in Samoa. I swam in the sea and I loved it here. I thought of my parents. I thought of my village. And I was happy. I was very happy to be back in Samoa.'

Pofitu's heart had been warmed, even during that first day, by the way the Samoan people had not changed. 'They were friendly and sharing,' she said. 'That's Samoan life. In Samoa you don't worry if you have no money because everybody will share with you. They will offer you a bed, they will offer you a house, they will feed you. That's the life of the Samoan people and it's a culture that they keep, even when they move away, even in Auckland. When Samoan people leave Samoa, they take with them their way of life of sharing with one another, helping one another. Everybody works together, helps each other, loves one another.'

Pofitu saw some changes, however. There were traffic lights in Apia. There never used to be. Now you could get pretty much anything you wanted at the shops and the market. There were televisions and radios, though there were still manual typewriters clacking in the bank. Pofitu thought most of the changes were for the better. She was pleased to see her Samoa progressing.

Of course other changes saddened her. 'My old friends, they were all gone. There was only the young generation now,' she said. But still, that was a mixed blessing. 'Even though I didn't know the young people, they smiled and said, "Hello, how are you?" We went shopping and the ladies were so welcoming. If you wanted them to sew you *lava lava* or a dress, they would do it straight away for you. Those kinds of things made me very happy: just the way the people were so friendly.'

Meanwhile, Jay had managed to break away from filming. But during the flight to Samoa reality hit, and he began mulling over their impending arrival in Samoa and what he'd got himself into. 'Firstly, I hoped my story would be interesting enough for a documentary,' he said. 'That was a real concern. Then there were thoughts of this whole idea of not being able to measure up as far as

Polynesia was concerned. We of the generation born speaking English as our first language always made fun of people who speak pigeon English, but thinking that I would go back there and they would judge me purely because I couldn't speak their language, that gave me the odd cold sweat on the trip over.'

Being the consummate all-round performer, Jay tried not to let any of that anxiety show for the camera when he and Matthew finally arrived. Of course, the way he clenched his jaw and furrowed his brow betrayed him. 'I put up so much falseness that I got there thinking, well, you know, the camera won't lie, the camera will shoot everything. They will go right into it. They'll go full tilt. I just felt inadequate.'

And it was too late to back out now.

Pofitu was at the airport to greet them. 'My son!' she exclaimed, hugging Jay hard, and he felt a little better about things. It was a relief to see his mum was so obviously happy to be there.

But before heading out of the airport, Jay retreated for a few minutes behind his very best line of defence, his can-do-man persona. 'Jay wears this bum bag,' said Eden. 'Whatever you need, it's in there: tissues, Band Aids, aspirin, toothpicks, chewing gum. He is this completely natural father and is constantly looking after people. You could see it in the way he would always have a hand on his mum's shoulder or looking over to make sure Matthew was okay. Even for me, as an adult,' Eden smiled, 'he was just a complete comfort to have around.' So at that moment Jay fussed about his mum and Matthew and anyone else who needed it, to avoid fussing about himself.

There would, however, be no chance of avoiding the fuss being made about Jay's arrival outside the airport. As soon as he set foot in Samoa, he found that the entire front page of the national newspaper was dedicated to him. 'Welcome Home Jay!' screamed the *Apia Times* headline. It ran in block letters down the side of a huge picture of Jay as Senior Constable Tommy Tavita, the character he played on *Water Rats*.

It wasn't like Jay had ever lived in Samoa and it wasn't like he'd come to Samoa to live, to shoot a movie or a TV show, or even to stay for an extended period. Yet his arrival was a big deal. The headline wasn't all that surprising, considering that outside sport, Jay was *the* most famous person of Samoan blood internationally. *Water Rats* was second only to the US medical drama, *ER*, in terms of the number of countries in which it was shown. Two hundred million people had seen *Water Rats* in 180 different countries – across Britain, Europe, the Middle East, Africa, Asia and the Pacific, including Indonesia, China and, of course, Samoa.

Jay was surprised and flattered by the coverage but didn't make a big deal of it. His travelling companions did, though – they gave him a right good ribbing. Jay took it good humouredly and with his usual confident graciousness. But the newspaper did nothing to settle his nerves.

There was no point in him dwelling on it, though. It was a Sunday and Jay, Pofitu and Matthew were off to church in Pofitu's village of Le ulumoega Tu ai. Naturally, everyone at church was curious about Jay. Women and girls wearing white frocks and fancy white hats smiled modestly. Men, in white *lava lava* and crisp bleached shirts remained dignified but obviously curious. Little girls in their white meringue dresses and little boys in their mini-*lava lava* and freshly ironed white shirts danced about on their bare feet outside the church and, once inside, sang a little louder, squirmed a little more and laughed more readily with Jay in their midst.

But here, Jay found his fears melting away. As a Christian man, he was moved by the experience of attending service in Samoa, where his parents' belief system, and his, had originated. And he looked down at Matthew, who was not afraid or uncomfortable. The boy was as curious about Samoan life as his hosts were about his father. Jay felt then that he had done the right thing in bringing Matthew and, in a rush of optimism about the trip, he thanked God for that.

After service, the children filed into the *fale* for Sunday School and sang their Christian songs so beautifully, it made Pofitu cry. Jay put his arm around her shoulder. This was her *'aiga*, his *'aiga* too.

In Samoa *'aiga*, or family, is everything. The bigger your extended family, the better. And the more powerful, even better. A powerful *'aiga* brings pride to its members. It also brings money. Pofitu left Samoa at the behest of her *'aiga*. She did not want to leave but her family needed her to. They wanted her to escape the poverty, the limited opportunities and lack of employment in Samoa. But never to escape *'aiga*. 'They said, go to look for your life over there. Go to help the family,' said Pofitu.

A good son or daughter of Samoa sent money back from America or Australia or New Zealand. In 1991 the census stated that seventy-five million New Zealand dollars came into Samoa from *'aiga* generosity, a good proportion of the gross domestic income. At the time the population of Samoa was less than two hundred thousand, and there was half that number again living in New Zealand, all sending back money, clothes and toys. Then there were between ten and twenty thousand Samoans in Australia, and about the same number in the United States, mostly in Hawaii and California.

At times Jay might have resented the obligatory contributions he had made to family in Samoa, but seeing those children at Sunday School in his mother's village, with his western child at his side, he felt more connected.

Here, in Samoa, Jay saw his mother in an entirely new context. He described this revelation with an unlikely but strangely apt analogy: 'I was asked to play in this celebrity AFL match at the SCG, and the former star league player, Mark "Jacko" Jackson was in the locker rooms with us before the match. He looked like a frail old pudgy man. And he winked at me and said, "Just stay with me, you'll be fine." We jog out through the tunnel and onto the field and in that time, this pudgy old man turned into a six foot seven warrior with this huge smile, and I could have sworn the years had just peeled back. My mother was the same in Samoa. The years peeled back and she was strong and beautiful. I wouldn't have believed it if I didn't see it. It was like seeing the young woman back on the islands.'

Jay was discovering things about his mother that could not be revealed anywhere but here. Outside the church there was what looked like an ordinary palm tree to Jay, but Pofitu was drawn to it and tears welled up in her eyes. 'What's the matter, Mum?' Jay asked.

'I love this tree. This is where my brother died.'

'And I asked her, "Well, why do you say I love this tree"?' Jay recounted. 'And she said, "Because there's always a memory here of my brother who should be with us today".' Jay had not heard this story before of how Pofitu's thirteen-year-old brother was play-fighting with friends when one of them hit him on the head with a piece of wood. Jay stood under the tree and thought, for the first time, about this uncle who was only four years older than Matthew when he died. And he thought about his mother as a young woman and the grief she must have endured at such a loss.

He was seeing Pofitu in her home before she was Nana, before she was Mum, before she was a wife. He saw her when she was Pofitu, happy in her village, her life still before her, an individual, not a figurehead.

He felt closer to her, to her history, to understanding the person he called Mum.

When Pofitu left her homeland, she had been *'aualuma*, an unmarried woman, at twenty-eight considered a late age to be single – nothing now in Australia and New Zealand, but in Samoa, and in 1958 . . .

'You must leave Samoa. You must go to New Zealand.

Go across the sea to help the family,' Pofitu remembered her father saying. Despite the fact that other Samoans had trodden this path to New Zealand before her, when Pofitu first arrived in Auckland she felt as if she were the only Samoan there. 'I went from Samoa to Fiji by boat, and plane from Fiji to New Zealand,' she remembered. 'I arrived on Guy Fawkes' night, and I tell you,' she sighed, 'I was really lonely. I cried and I wanted to go back to Samoa, and I said to myself, "I don't know what I'm doing here." I looked at a photo of my family and it made me so homesick. I was really sad. But I said to myself, "Well, I can't start feeling better if I just go on like this, crying and missing my family," so I made a big effort to change. I went and looked for a job and I got one.'

Pofitu was smart, well-educated and a nurse. In Apia, she had earned five pounds a month. In Auckland, at St Helen's Hospital, she was earning twenty-three pounds a fortnight. By going away, she had become a big help to her *'aiga*.

'With a job, I began to be happier,' said Pofitu.

Still, it took her a while to find her feet. Pofitu had come from a place where passionfruit and guava, coconuts, breadfruit and bananas grew freely, and where the staple of most meals was succulent pork, freshly slaughtered there in the village. Children ate sugar cane, not lollies, and men smoked the rough Samoan tobacco rolled in newspaper.

In comparison, Auckland felt so foreign and so far away from all that she loved. While Apia had maybe eight shops, Auckland seemed to have a world of them.

New Zealand did not have village life and, despite its islander heritage, it had a faraway Queen and white people ways – and cheese in cardboard packets and Tupperware and electrical goods and Marlboro.

But Pofitu never lost sight of why she had come to Auckland: to work and do well for her *'aiga*. The foundation of her resolve was her faith in God, a faith that was closely entwined with her work ethic and the history of her people. When the Christian missionaries had first come to Samoa in 1830, they appeared to be living proof of the prophecy of the great Samoan warrior queen, Nafanua, that a new religion would arrive and so end the rule of the old gods. Samoa had readily converted to Christianity and the riches of the church had been seen as a sign of the potency of what they preached. From that time onwards working for the *palagi*, the white people, had become a way for Samoans to share in that wealth.

Pofitu came from a nation of courageous people. Twelve hundred years before the Vikings crossed the Atlantic Ocean, Pofitu's forebears had crossed tracts of open ocean in canoes, reaching as far as South America. Samoans were also fiercely independent people: they had welcomed the *palagi* to their shores, but had always resisted imperial oppression. It was eye-opening for Pofitu to see the indigenous Maoris often excluded socially and economically in white-dominated New Zealand. While they might have been poor, her compatriots back home in Samoa were a majority and gathering strength in their struggle for political independence, which they would ultimately win in 1962. Of course,

Pofitu was well aware that the *palagi* who lived in Samoa were richer than the Samoans – it seemed *palagi* were always richer – but freedom was priceless.

Faith, courage and independence were in Pofitu's blood, and gradually her life in Auckland fell into place. However, something was missing: a suitable eligible bachelor.

'When I got to New Zealand, there were hardly any Samoan boys,' said Pofitu. 'We were not looking to the *palagi* men because we did not understand the *palagi* way.' Then she became reacquainted with Finauga. She had met him when she was a child; he was a little older than she, and would come to her school to help an aunt who cleaned there.

Pofitu married Finauga, a good man, a religious man and a hard man – a Samoan of his generation. Six children came along and in the middle of them was Jay. It was Tui first, then Ualesi, then Jay, Kilisimasi, Sepola and Finuaga – or Chris, Deborah and Frank, as the last three were known. Pofitu had succeeded in all her aspirations; she had done very well for her *'aiga*.

But now, standing on the front lawn of the church in the village where she grew up, all the layers of her life fell away, all those years of being a New Zealand citizen, wife, mum and nana. Here, right here, in Samoa, she could really be Samoan first.

Pofitu was so proud to bring her famous son back to her village. 'For a long time my father's village got the credit for having this actor, this performer as one of theirs,' said Jay. 'All of a sudden, my mother's people clued into the fact that I was also part of their village.'

Their enthusiasm was a gift to Pofitu – a gift the village had helped Jay give her. And so he wanted to give something back to the village. But in wanting to do that, the old reservations and fears resurfaced: fears of being found out a coconut, memories of being an outsider on that first trip to Samoa in 1990, feeling that he didn't belong, feeling inadequate because his language skills weren't up to speed.

'Not being a fluent speaker of Samoan is always a hurdle for me and a personal embarrassment, purely because I understand what is being said but then when I go to verbalise, I may as well be speaking Mandarin,' he said.

But for his mum, his *'aiga* and himself, he just had to get over the anxiety and embarrassment to give the gift he really wanted to give. He decided to run a kind of theatre sports meets *Playschool* session for the children.

'I promised the minister's wife that I would come back to the village and run a workshop, just a couple of hours, for the kids. I don't know what they thought a workshop was. But I just wanted to see some of the relations come and, you know, have a play in a constructive, learning way that encouraged thinking and creativity. We thought maybe thirty of the young people would turn up. We got there and there were one hundred and thirty people,' said Jay, remembering the wide smiles, the eager, excited faces, the carefree bare feet on cool green grass, the giggles and shouts. And he remembered his own emotions, the rising nervousness, then the excitement and finally, the exultation, like the first time he was ever on stage.

'I asked, "Hands up all those who can speak English",' he said. 'There were four people who put up their hand.'

But it didn't matter, he discovered. The language barrier *was* no barrier. He could indeed have been speaking Mandarin if he wanted to. They played simple games, and the communion of enthusiasm and love transcended language and fear. Mostly.

'Okay!' said Jay to his workshop participants in his limited Samoan: 'Get in different lines of ten. Now get into the order of height without talking.' The kids merrily muddled through the exercise. 'Now in order of your birthday.

'And I got them to do exercises with numbers, where each had to respond to their particular assigned number when I called it out,' Jay recalled. 'I said a Samoan word, which I thought was the word for "eleven", but I actually said "seven". And so they responded to seven, and I was all confused, going, "No, that's . . . No . . . Oh, okay." And my mother was sitting there muttering, going, "Count on your fingers if you have to".' He imitated her disdain and laughed. 'And at one stage I shouted out what I thought was a number and she said, "That's food." So I'm shouting "Spaghetti!" for no apparent reason and they're all going, "What? What?"' Jay laughed.

Though Pofitu frowned at him and shook her head, inside she laughed, too. She was so proud of her son, thrilled to see him give so much of himself to his family.

'We left there late. They said you must be very tired. But I said, "We have always gifted these people money. This is what else I have." Giving money was par for the course. I wanted to give something more meaningful, something of myself, I suppose. So an acting workshop was all I could give. It was very humbling. It wasn't so much for them as for my mum really, to say: "My mum has come back to her village. You have welcomed her back and therefore as the son of Pofitu, I give this to you".'

In Samoa water is believed to be the cradle of existence. And now it was the water that helped Matthew open up to Samoa. Jay took him to Papase'ea, the sliding rock, where water has cascaded down through lush forest foliage since time immemorial, smoothing the granite beneath its path and making it ideal for catapulting down into the cool, fresh pool below.

Sliding and splashing about with Matthew in the pristine pool surrounded by Samoan forest, Jay felt like a Samoan father. He showed his son how to split coconut and shred it in the traditional way; they walked barefoot together, breathed in the ocean breeze and felt the warmth of the sun on their skin together.

It didn't take long for Matthew to ditch his Gameboy. 'The first day I was playing my Gameboy,' said Matthew. 'The second day I was like, "Oh, who needs Gameboy? Let me get out there!"'

'Matthew didn't want to leave Samoa,' said Pofitu proudly. 'Oh, he loved the water, the sea. He loved going down the slide with his father. He was really happy. And I said, "One day, we will be back again in Samoa." And that made him happy. He loved it.'

And that made Pofitu happy, too. Matthew's joy was another gift to her.

Jay, Pofitu and Matthew travelled across the island of Upolu to the remote village of Vavāu in the hope of seeing Pofitu's beloved older sister, Māsāga. Now eighty-two, Māsāga had moved to Vavāu to live with her husband and, though he was long gone, she had remained there ever since. Pofitu had not seen her sister in more than twenty-eight years.

'I want to see her before one of us dies,' Pofitu told Eden.

Driving to Vavāu, Pofitu played guide, pointing out landmarks and places of interest along the way. But her mind was filled with anticipation. 'When we arrived in Apia, I was trying to think of ways to let her know we were coming before we went to see her,' said Pofitu. 'But there was no way to contact her. So she did not know we were coming. On our way there, we passed some people walking on the road and we asked them if they knew where she was.'

They directed her to a small, traditional *fale* with a red tiled roof instead of thatching, but no walls, just supporting beams leading up from the floor, raised from the earth in case of flood and to keep the structure cool. Inside, they found Māsāga sitting on uncovered mattresses, her belongings stacked in suitcases behind her. She was thin, her grey hair fine and wispy around her creviced face, her eyes milky from cataracts. Two young village girls stood by Māsāga, gently waving pandanus fans to cool her, as was the Samoan way – elders have always been respected and looked after by the younger generation.

The true meaning of homecoming – Pofitu's sister, Māsāga, weeps with joy

'I called out to her,' said Pofitu, weeping softly at the memory, 'And she goes to me, "Who, who, who is that?" like that, because she couldn't see. And when I mentioned my name, *it's me, Pofitu . . .*' Pofitu's voice trailed off, she was weeping so much.

At the sound of the name Pofitu, Māsāga immediately raised her arms and the two women embraced and cried. For Pofitu, this was the true meaning of homecoming, the embrace of *'aiga*, the total acceptance that made the years away dissolve.

Pofitu, still strong and robust, held her frail sister and wept silently, listening as Māsāga told her between sobs, 'It's been such a long time. I have been praying for this moment. And I thought I would be dead before I would get the chance to see you again.'

Māsāga hugged her sister around the neck, burying her head in Pofitu's shoulder. Through her tears she continued, 'Last week while I was praying, I saw a vision of my mother in front of me. I tried to ask her, "What are you doing here?" And as I started to talk to her, she walked outside. As she went, I was able to call out to her, "*Fue*, are you going to go again? Why did you come?" Now I know why she came to me, to tell me the wonderful news that my sister would be coming to see me.'

Jay looked to Matthew to make sure he was okay witnessing such an achingly emotional scene. But Matthew was fine. And when Māsāga finally calmed herself enough to kiss him hello, Matthew embraced her with all the warmth, love and respect that was the essence of being Samoan.

As they left Māsāga's home, Jay and Matthew hugged Pofitu. Two Samoan men making sure their elder was okay.

Jay comforts Pofitu as she leaves her sister's house

Jay's father's village of Fa'ala Palauli on the big island of Savai'i, was only a short ferry ride from 'Upolu, across calm South Pacific water. But for Jay it would be his biggest journey yet. This was where he would have to follow in the footsteps of his father, Finauga, and show his own son not only what it was to be Samoan, but what it meant to be a Laga'aia. This was where all Jay's insecurities, doubts and conflicts over identity surfaced, because he was not sure if he would be accepted as Samoan by his father's people. For Jay, it was time to find out whether or not he measured up. No amount of fussing over his mother and son could stave off Jay's anxiety. There was a lot riding on this visit, and it wasn't just about Jay; it was about his ability to strengthen the bonds of Samoa and Laga'aia in his family beyond this trip.

Jay said, 'I want to be able to stand there as my father's son and be able to pass on stories to my children, to be able to pass on an idea of who I really am and to pass on the passion, I suppose, for being a Polynesian.'

Jay believed he was bringing up his children well. He was teaching them what they needed to do to succeed in their world. They knew, or would know, he said, that education was important, that putting your hand up with an answer in class was a way to get along in a world that was dominated by white people. 'Too many Polynesians, when white people knock on the door, either hide under the table because they think they are Jehovah's Witnesses or because they think they've come to arrest them or collect money they don't have. I need my children to know how to survive in the white world, but I also want them to know what it is to be Polynesian. It's hard trying to keep one foot in each world. It's something I have tried to do. But maybe the Samoan side of things has suffered.'

And he worried that it would show when he got to Fa'ala, that perhaps his father's people might have good reason to believe he wasn't a 'proper Samoan'. In some ways he knew it was true, that there were certain aspects of his Samoan heritage he could not fulfil because of who he was and where he lived.

When Jay's father Finauga died, Jay became a *matai*, a chief, just like his father had been. There are two types of chiefs in Samoan society: one is God given, the spiritual chief, handed down in a certain strain of lineage; the other is *tulafale* and that chief is appointed. Jay carried the *matai* title of *tulafale*, the orator chief. He was bestowed with this title because he was the one with the gift of oration. In Samoan tradition, you don't have to be the oldest to be *tulafale*, the *'aiga* chooses their man by consensus. The Laga'aias agreed that their man was the middle child, Jay, because the *matai* title of *tulafale*, the orator chief, suited him. He spoke strong and proud – in English anyway.

Pofitu wanted Jay to fulfil his *matai* role and get the traditional tattoos, the marks of who he was: a Samoan chieftain. Jay said he couldn't get the tattoos. If he did, people might think he was in a gang or something. Those tattoos might limit his work opportunities. And his title would then become a curse rather than a blessing.

But still, the decision not to get them weighed on him. 'I am the plastic Polynesian, you know,' he said. 'People say, you should go and do your chieftains properly. But to have a proper chieftain ceremony in Savai'i, to receive this, you have to have full tattoos. What the tattoos symbolise is that you are passing into another stage of responsibility and this is a mark of the commitment you will make, that you are serving your village. I'd love to get an armband, but in my profession I can't afford it. I live here, in the Western world. I don't live there in Samoa, and as much as you would like to carry on that tradition . . . well, that's where you're torn.'

Jay had always been torn, it seemed. Well before his father died, Jay was torn between his parents' wishes and his need to fulfil his own ambitions.

'"Stay," I told him,' said Pofitu of Jay's early days as a performer, when he was really only beginning to explore his potential. 'But he wanted to go with these three Maori boys to sing in Sydney and Brisbane. He did that but when he came back to Auckland I said to him, "Don't you ever go with those boys again." But he said, "Mum, I want to go with them".'

'My husband and I felt he belonged at home. We kept trying to stop him but he said, "It's my life and I love singing." I always called him a big mouth and I got mad and never let him sing. But then I said in my heart, "If he really wants to do things like that, if he is happy to do things in front of people, if he won't stop, well, it must be his life." And it was. It was his life. So finally he asked me if he could go and do some other thing, so I say, "Okay. You go and do it. And if you go, keep going forward, not back again".'

Jay had been going forward ever since. It seemed inevitable that he would; he'd always been a tearaway kid, a little different.

'As the third eldest and fourth youngest, you are basically in the twilight zone unless you smash something,' said Jay. 'But I was always the creative one. I was always running scams in my head; always something going on, never able to sit still. Yeah, I was the fence jumper in this family and had to trailblaze my way through. The worst part of doing that was not knowing exactly where I was going but knowing I had to go *that* way. And you learn philosophies along the way. I always tell kids now, sometimes you have to go sideways to go forward. Just because you're pumping gas somewhere or chopping down trees, doesn't mean you're not going to achieve your goals. Sometimes you've just got to take care of business.'

Taking care of business was a philosophy Finauga had understood well – though Jay and his father had certainly gone about their business in very different ways.

Finauga had worked as a storeman for Watties. He worked hard in the factory providing for his children, his wife and his *'aiga* back in Samoa. And he did not tolerate any nonsense.

Jay remembered his father coming home from work one night and finding no salt on the dinner table. 'I work a hundred and forty hours a day. I only have one pair of pants. You think you could put the salt on the table. What, are you saving it for someone else?' Jay imitated his dad. Then all the Laga'aia children would point at each other, accusing each other of being at fault, their voices high, their speech quick. Their dad would often find something amiss. Maybe the butter would not be on the table. Maybe the bread wouldn't be. And maybe Jay would hide something or other, just to push his dad's buttons. His brothers would kick Jay under the table. '*Jay*!' they'd hiss. 'What are you doing? Put it back.' But it would be too late. Their father would have noticed. 'I work hard to put bread on this table and there is no bread on this table.' And sometimes they might all cop a clip across the ear because of Jay's prank.

Of course, it wasn't always Jay starting the trouble. None of the Laga'aia kids were angels, but they weren't all bad either. They might have been streetwise but they were brought up to love Christ and their parents, too. They were God-fearing and parent-fearing. All the Samoan kids they knew were. Their parents were big and strong, proud and traditional and devoutly Christian. Their parents might have left Samoa, but they'd brought Samoa with them. The way things were done by their parents and their parents' parents and all who went before was the way they demanded things be done now. Sure, in New Zealand Jay had pop music and television, Western schooling and magazines, blue jeans and Nike – and dreams of being a performer. But there was order in the *'aiga*, always.

'Come here, boy,' Finauga would say when Jay was in trouble. The patriarch would be sitting stone-faced in his chair across the other side of the lounge room. 'He wouldn't move. You'd have to go to him. That's the Samoan parent way. They don't move, they make you come to them,' Jay laughed. But when he was a boy and his dad said, 'Come here, boy,' Jay would start to shake. Up and down the street, someone's dad was saying, 'Come here, boy,' and a boy would be shaking.

'When it came to discipline, my father wasn't one to muck around. He adopted an Al-Pacino-meets-Bruce-Lee type of method,' said Jay. 'He would sit down and then he would ask you a question, an open-ended question, and then he would wait. "Why? . . . Why?"' Jay imitated his father's almost whispered question, full of disappointment and impending doom.

' "Why what, Dad?"

' "You know, I tell you, and still you go and do it."

'And you're like, "Oh shit, I should've read up on this one." You're just standing there, and all of a sudden the doors go . . .' Jay intimated with his hands and breath the sight and sound of doors slamming suddenly, all by themselves. Like in the Bruce Lee movies. 'And everyone disappears, the house quietens, and in the distance, a wolf howls,' Jay laughed. 'And then my father would go, "You know, I work, I come here, I don't want to hear this."

'And then you think, does he know about the glass I smashed last year? And you have no idea whether or not one of your brothers has dobbed you in for something they've done, so you think, I'm not owning up to anything until he commits himself. And then he would throw a box of matches at me – he was a heavy smoker – and it would hit me and then I'd stand there thinking to myself, does he think it's heavier than it really is? Should I play the impact, or should I just stand here and start to cry? And then he'd just go, "Bring it here." And then he'd go, "Put it down here." And you'd hold the very edge of the box of matches with your fingers, stretch your arm out as much as possible to be as far away as possible from him, and he'd be watching all the time. And then he'd go, "What's the matter? Put it down here." And you're just about to put it down and the next thing you know, he's faked with one hand and played it with the other hand and all you hear is . . .' Jay made the unmistakeable sound of a clip across the ear.

When dinner was finished and the table was cleared, the Laga'aia children would sit in a circle in the lounge room, their father at the centre. Everyone would have a copy of the Samoan Bible and the children would fidget nervously as Finauga would look fiercely around the gathering. Each child would have to read a passage from the Bible in Samoan. 'And you'd do stuff like, you'd count around so you knew which verse you were getting,' said Jay. 'And you'd run it through in your head because, you know, he'd read fluently and it'd be your turn and you'd be stammering and stumbling . . . and you knew you were just going to get abused. And after we'd all finished the prayers, we'd all go "Amen" and the lights would come back on and we'd bolt for the door and he'd go, "*Stop!*"

'Damn it, we were nearly away. But you'd sigh, turn around and get ready for it: "You speak the English, but you don't know your own language," and it went on and on.'

Jay's experiences growing up were by no means unique, though. At twilight, Samoan boys across the neighbourhood would be sneaking off to play basketball, hoping to meld into the shadows, undetected in the dimness. *Thwap!* A rubber thong hurled from a doorstep might land at their feet, or maybe hit one of them. They would freeze. 'And all the brothers would turn around and all the cousins would turn around and go, "It's your mum's, man. I recognise that size twelve anywhere",' said Jay. 'And the whisper would go around, "That's not my mum's." "That's not my mum's." "We can still go. We can still go to the park." And then the worst part of it was, if it was your mum's, your younger brothers or your older brothers would go, "I didn't see that happen, therefore it's only affected you because you saw it".' He laughed. 'And then you'd hear, "BRING – IT – BACK!" yelled from a nearby porch.'

Jay would bring the thong back to his mum and when he handed it over he'd get a clip across the ear with it and be commanded inside. But the following night or the next time they'd try to sneak off, it would be someone else's mum's shoe or thong. The memory of those times made him laugh.

Jay, however, does not use shoes as missiles on his kids. He kisses them and tells them how proud he is of them and listens to their stories when they slip into their look-at-me routines. But he brings authority to bear when he needs to.

'Sometimes I hear myself, and I am my father,' he said, with a far-off look and a smile of deep pride and recognition at that connection with his father, at the father in them both. He smiled, too, because the strength and confidence in his own voice that had made him not only *tulafale*, but an actor, had come from his father. And that gift for speaking seemed to encapsulate all that was different and all that was shared between father and son.

'My mother always says I was a great foil for my father because he was a great orator and he would study so that he knew the traditions of the different villages,' said Jay. 'He could stand at formal meetings and just rattle off, ". . . the son of so-and-so who came from so-and-so" and on and on. He knew all the lineages and stories. Stories from all the villages. He spoke in Samoan so well but his

English wasn't as good, so I would cover from that end.'

Recalling his father's stories made Jay miss him and wish he'd listened more to his dad. But his dad didn't talk that much to his adult children.

'Mum would always say, "Your dad's very proud of you; very proud of you",' said Jay. 'I always thought, why couldn't he say it then?'

When Jay began singing in Auckland clubs at the age of fifteen, his dad would come and watch. 'My mother would be there, too, with my aunties, all smiling, and I would see my father saying to people around him, "My son, my son," but he would never say anything to me.'

Jay left home two years later at seventeen. 'I fell out with my father,' he said simply. 'I left and went out into the world and then in '83 he got cancer. Just before he died he got what my brother calls the faraway eyes, and he called for me. He had never called for anybody. And I got to say goodbye. I got there, saw him, we slept and through that night he died.'

Finauga Laga'aia might have passed away, but for Jay, his father's presence remains real and alive in his own heart, in his face and in his words. And as Jay prepared for the trip to Fa'ala he was never more conscious of the weight of Finauga's legacy and what it meant to carry it on.

But there was a gift waiting for Jay in Fa'ala.

When Jay stepped into his father's village, all his pent up anxiety flew away on the warm breeze. The Laga'aia cousins, uncles, aunties and everyone else in the extended *'aiga* had gathered to greet Jay, Pofitu and Matthew, and the feasting began. The young girls wore flowers behind their ears, the men their best *lava lava*. Sure, Jay's fame was something to celebrate, but first and foremost he was being welcomed as Finauga's son.

A gathering of the Lagaʻaia ʻaiga at Jay's father's ancestral home

In the midst of this welcome, truth hit home for Jay. 'They accepted me for who I am. They didn't expect me to speak Samoan any better than I did, they didn't expect me to be anything that I wasn't. They appreciated the fact that I was there; the simple fact that the son had come home.'

Jay's feelings of inadequacy had been his alone, and the realisation was liberating.

As Jay walked through the village plantation with his cousin Lalatoa and heard stories of his father, he realised he had played an important role in the workings of the plantation. While they talked, Jay noted his cousin's talon-like fingernails – he'd kept them long for his guitar playing. Jay remembered that his father had also kept his fingernails long for mandolin playing – the one extravagance this practical man had maintained throughout his life for the sake of music. In this place Jay could hear his father play and hear his words again. Jay recognised that he was Laga'aia *tulafale*. And watching his own son Matthew taking it all in, chatting and bouncing around and clearly feeling in his element, Jay could see he was probably Laga'aia *tulefale* material, too.

For Matthew, his skin now glowing from the Samoan sun, the trip to Fa'ala was a highlight. 'We own a plantation and we own a beach,' Matthew said later of the village and '*aiga* property. 'Going with Daddy there was really cool. They all know who he is. In Sydney, everyone is used to famous people. In Samoa, they go crazy at my dad!' Although these were nine-year-old Matthew's most striking impressions of Samoa – the reaction to his dad, the waterfall, the blowholes and the beach – Jay hoped that this trip had planted the seeds for his son's deeper understanding and respect for his '*aiga*.

'Now Matthew knows where his father comes from and that's a good thing,' said Pofitu. 'Matthew knows where all the Laga'aia fathers come from. He can see the

Samoan way of life and he will know and understand when he grows up that it is good. And he will know who he is and that is good because in New Zealand they say to Matthew that Jay is a Maori, and in Australia they say he is an Aborigine. But now Matthew knows his father is a real black Samoan.'

As the sun set on their final night in Samoa, Jay, Pofitu and Matthew were back at Aggie Grey's Hotel where musicians played Samoan music and sang romantic and joyful songs. Jay and Pofitu danced and Pofitu mused that she might come back to Samoa to live. Jay thought his mother looked so beautiful, so happy and refreshed, that the trip had been worth it for this alone.

Jay knew he wouldn't be coming back to Samoa to live any time soon. His life was elsewhere. But something of his lifeblood was also here and he was grateful to have had the opportunity to understand that better.

'The Samoans, they are hard-working people, people of the land, and what always struck me was there was a juxtaposition between the beautiful scenery and beautiful beaches and the poverty,' he said. 'It always saddened me.

'But the sense of community overrides all that and the family structure is the glue that binds them together. And it is that glue that I have found binding me to them. The glue that I thought ran in the veins of our family runs in the veins of all the brown skins. We are all matriarchal – the men tend to go out and forage, but at the end of the day, it is our women folk, our mothers, who say when we go and when we stay and probably until my mum goes to see my dad, it will be that way.' He laughed. 'And then my sister Deborah will probably take over!'

After the trip to Samoa, Jay felt an even stronger sense of family – if that were possible for the Laga'aia clan – and he would see to it that there would at least be a gathering of the Laga'aia *'aiga* in Auckland soon.

'Though the thing is,' he said, 'you have another reunion, another tearful reunion and then you go, "We really have to meet up. You know, we have to have an event." And the unfortunate thing about it is, you go, "We're having a party, we want everyone to come," you know, you invite the family and no one shows up. But if it's someone's funeral, they all feel obliged to turn up. So I'm thinking about pretending someone's died to get everyone together. I'll tell them the truth after everyone's arrived. It will probably be a good party after the chairs stop being thrown!'

There are also plans to go back to Samoa soon. Very big plans. Back in Auckland Pofitu said, 'My two sons, Ualesi and Chris, they have never been to Samoa, only Jay, Tui, Frank and Deborah. But Frank was in Samoa really young. Now, after our trip, they are all dying to go to Samoa. They really want to go.'

'I've been nagging Dad for us all to return to Samoa ever since we got back,' said Matthew.

'Now the whole family talks of going back,' said Pofitu. 'Matthew says, "What about Daddy?" I go, "Daddy's all right. We'll go back without him".' She laughed. But now some of the Laga'aias were thinking seriously of moving to Samoa.

'I am getting old now. I could go back to the island. In my heart, I really want us to go back there. My family, they see that I was very happy there and they want to go,' said Pofitu. 'I didn't think I would see my village or my people or my husband's village in this time of my life. I had given up on going back. But I saw my sister and I saw all those other relatives and I thank God because, though God loves us, you don't know when bad things will happen. So when we went to Samoa, I said, "Well, I think that is a gift from God to me." We gave thanks to God for this trip to Samoa.'

Jay's prayer of thanks was deep and heartfelt. He had gained so much himself by going to Samoa, but the happiness the trip had given his mother transcended everything.

'I can clearly mark the earth-moving events in my life,' said Jay. 'The first time I saw my wife, my marriage, the birth of each of my children. The first time I was offered a lead of a show, the first time I realised I didn't suck. But for Mum, her benchmarks basically stopped when my dad died. There were movements in the forest as far as grandchildren being born, a collection of those moments. But this trip was something that was innately her. This was her being her and had nothing to do with her offspring. It was about her coming home.

'We are Samoan. We are Laga'aia and we know full well that her home is where her family is, but every time she talks about Samoa and her return, there is an inner glow now. On her sixtieth birthday, she went to Jerusalem, to Bethlehem and saw these places, these Christian places that meant so much to her. It was a once in a lifetime trip for her. But for her to go home to Auckland and say that this topped the trip to Bethlehem in the sense that she was able to connect with her roots, well, it really fulfilled everything for her. I don't know that she will move back. There are grandchildren in Australia and New Zealand. We can't all move to Samoa. And her being in Samoa would make it harder for her to see us all. But isn't it just brilliant; the trip was so special, that she'd even think of moving back. The Samoa in her heart was enriched, and that's the absolute best result.'

Jay mulled it over. He remembered when Eden first called him about the journey back to Samoa. He remembered how so many thoughts came rushing to the fore about his mother. Was Pofitu strong enough for the trip? Would she cope with the heat? Would she cope with the emotion of it all? And he remembered the threats from his brothers and sisters. *If anything happens to Mum . . .* Things happened all right. Wonderful, liberating, inspiring things.

A zest for life fuels my journey . . .

And my journey fuels my zest for life.

PAN HAN-LIANG

Cindy Pan
Chinese Australian

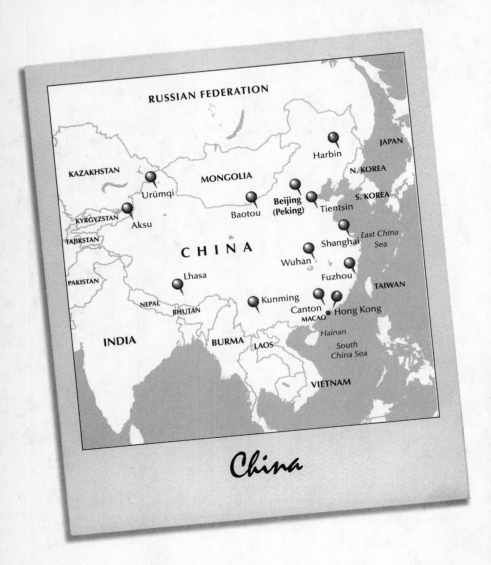

China

Dancing with Strangers

'People look at you and know you're Chinese. You always know you're Chinese. Sometimes it's negative. But sometimes, it's like knowing you're a woman; it's not necessarily bad. Like you're a woman with a group of men, you're just not the same.'

Cindy Pan's face is one of the most recognisable Asian faces on Australian television. A TV medico, she has dispensed advice laced with her unique, kooky sense of humour as a regular guest on Australian television talk shows like *The Panel* and *Beauty and the Beast*. She usually presents herself as anything but the serious medical type, and has broken the traditional image of the conservative Chinese GP. Yet despite being a role model for Chinese–Australian success, Cindy Pan had never been to the land of her forebears.

So when Eden Gaha approached Cindy about travelling to China with her mother, the idea had instant appeal. While Cindy's sense of her Chinese identity was a fact of her everyday life, it was something that remained incomplete for her.

Every day of her childhood growing up in Australia, Cindy was reminded that she was Chinese. It wasn't just the face in the mirror in the morning or the faces and stories of her parents that informed young Cindy of it. 'At school, everyone was constantly telling me, "Oh, you're Chinese; you're a ching-chong." How could I not know I was Chinese?'

Cindy and her brother David were the sole Chinese kids in a 1970s schoolyard sea of Anglo–Europeans. They were forerunners of the changing face of twenty-first century Australia, but back there at her suburban Sydney school, Cindy didn't know things were going to change, that faces similar to hers would become commonplace in the Australian schoolyard. She just knew that she and her brother were different and that their kind of different was far from positive. She clearly recalled kids in the playground chanting at her, *Chinese, Japanese, goodness gracious what are these?*

And the embarrassment of the lunch box. It was Dymo-taped with her name: 'Cindy H.L. Pan'. She lived in constant worry that someone would ask her about that 'H.L.'. 'People would ask me, "What does the H.L. stand for?" And I would really want to say Helen Louise or something. But you know how you just can't tell lies when you're young? I'd say, regretfully, "Oh, it stands for Han-

Liang. That's my Chinese name." My brother David's is Han-Kwang. And they'd go "Huh?" And you'd just think, oh here we go,' Cindy laughed. 'You just didn't want to go there. Having a Chinese name and an Australian name made you feel you had two lives: in public or at school you wouldn't use the name that your parents called you, or the names you called each other at home.

'When I was little I used to fantasise about growing up somewhere where everyone was Chinese,' she said, smiling. 'I thought that would be really good because I thought I wouldn't suffer any racism then.'

As an adult, she was still being reminded of her cultural heritage, though now in positive ways. An accomplished woman of many talents – medical doctor, actor, dancer, broadcaster and writer – she was a Chinese–Australian success story with a media profile at a time when Chinese-descended celebrities of any kind, let alone TV personalities, were rare in Australia. In addition to this, the Chinese community in Australia had embraced Cindy, conferring on her the honour of official spokesperson duties.

The most obvious reminder of Cindy's heritage remained the basic, inescapable fact of genetics: her eyes, her hair, her skin. 'People look at you and know you're Chinese,' said Cindy. 'You always know you're Chinese. Sometimes it's negative. But sometimes, it's like knowing you're a woman; it's not necessarily bad. Like you're a woman with a group of men, you're just not the same.'

Cindy's mother Ching-Lee agreed. 'It's simple things like friends saying to me, "I wouldn't dream of going out and having a Chinese meal unless you're there. I wouldn't know what to order." They're not being mean to me. My friends are very good to me. It's just a very, very subtle reminder of a difference,' she said.

'Being Chinese is a million things,' said Cindy. 'It's an impossible-to-extract element of your identity. It's something you live with your whole life. Even before we went to school I knew that we were different to everyone else and that we were Chinese. You didn't see many Chinese people about but if you did you'd notice it. Whenever you saw Chinese people in real life or in pictures or rarely on TV or in a movie – sometimes we'd see movies at the Chinese Consulate – you were constantly putting it together. Oh, so that's what Chinese people are like. That's how they behave. That's what they do. And then when you were a bit older, say a teenager, and you actually knew Chinese people of your own age, you knew Chinese parents were a certain way. So you gradually built up this whole library of information of what it was to be Chinese, what it was to be Chinese in Australia, at a physical level, in respect of what you're supposed to be good at and how you're supposed to behave, and all these kinds of things. And then at uni, there were lots of Chinese people and you were a particular faction of the Chinese community, that is, for me, the Chinese medical student which is quite a strongly identifiable group. And then I guess it was just finding your identity within all that. And everything that you found out about Chinese people, at the beginning, could be a bit intimidating, because you think, oh, does that mean I'm like that?'

Despite all these constant reinforcements of her origins, for better or worse, she was still haunted by the thought: 'I'm not a proper Chinese person, really.'

Part of this stemmed from looking like a Chinese person but not speaking Chinese.

When Cindy's mother Ching-Lee came to Australia, she understood little English. Her family had migrated from China and went first to Indonesia, where Ching-Lee and her sister Ching-May learned some English from a Dutch nun. 'She spoke English with a very strong Dutch accent, so when I came to Australia and sat in the classroom, I thought, this doesn't sound like English at all,' Ching-Lee laughed. 'It was very difficult but the headmaster was very nice. The day I started he called two girls from the class that I was to join, and told them, "I want you to look after Ching-Lee," and they did. They sat on either side of me and they literally, bodily took me to each class and they were very good. Of course, being girlfriends, they ended up talking across me because I guess they missed each other. So after a while I said, "Look, I'll look after myself," which I did. But it was very hard. So when I began to learn English in Australia, I let the Chinese go. I used to be able to read the newspaper and I no longer can. And I have been going to Chinese class for over five years now and I still can't read the newspaper,' she laughed.

In the 1950s Ching-Lee's diplomat father led the family to Australia. They were refugees at the time when Chairman Mao took over China and when the White Australia Policy was still a lingering force in the attitudes of Australians. Ching-Lee does not specify the traumas of being a Chinese child in post-World War Two Australia; instead, she refers to the time in vague terms as having been 'very hard' or 'quite difficult', occasionally delving as deep as 'very bad' and sometimes 'horrible'. Almost half a century in Australia had given her many Australian traits, but Ching-Lee's understatement of her experience of racism reflected a common Chinese response. 'Chinese people are always very keen to save face, so you always present the best things to your guests,' she said.

Cindy has a similar stoicism. She often laughs or makes some quip when touching on issues of racism and identity. Ching-Lee might have passed that trait on to Cindy, but she and her husband had been determined from the beginning not to pass on to their children things that would make their life in a white, English-speaking world difficult. Their first priority had been to make sure their children's English was as good as that of the blond, blue-eyed kid next door.

'At the time we were very friendly with this couple who had two children three years older than my two children and they only spoke to those children in Cantonese,' said Ching-Lee. 'So when they went to school those children didn't speak any English and they had a terrible time – much, much worse than I did because at least I had some English; they didn't have any. They had such a bad time. Academically they never really caught up. So I thought, this is not what I am going to do to my kids. Being the only Chinese children at the school, I didn't want them standing in the corner of the schoolyard not having anyone to talk to, and not understanding a thing of what was going on in class. So I decided to teach them English.'

For Cindy, the move paid off. Academically, she shone, going on to graduate in medicine. Artistically she also blossomed. Ballet became one of her great passions – she did classical dance to the Intermediate stage with the Royal Academy of Dance and was principal dancer in the Tony Award-winning production of *The King and I*, which toured Australia in 1991 and '92. As little as four years ago she was still dancing and performing in the theatre.

Cindy also enjoys acting. It's hard enough for anyone to break into acting, but when you have an Asian face opportunities can be even more scarce. Yet Cindy worked professionally, featuring in television, film and stage roles. The combination of her great sense of humour, medical background and ease with performance metamorphosed into a role as a popular media medico. And all the while, she practised as a GP from her clinic, first in Sydney's inner city, then on Sydney's North Shore.

In 1999 she was offered the prestigious role of Ambassador for Chinese New Year for the City of Sydney, a role she continues still. Cindy is also often invited to speak at Chinese–Australian events, and is proud and honoured to do that kind of work, to be a part of the Australian–Chinese community. Cindy said such roles opened her eyes further to her cultural heritage. Yet when she attended those official occasions, it was then that she felt most sharply the notion that she wasn't a real Chinese person.

She felt like a fraud because of the very thing that had contributed to her success in Australia – learning English at the expense of Chinese.

Cindy Pan could not write or read Chinese. She was not a fluent Chinese speaker. In fact, she spoke and understood very little Chinese.

'I have been to lots of Chinese functions where I can't understand what they're talking about,' said Cindy; 'They're all laughing and you don't know what they're laughing about. Even just not being able to read signs; I went to this Chinese dinner once, I was the MC for President Jiang Zemin's reception, and all the name cards on the dinner table were written in Chinese. It was like a bad dream. People said, "You can find your table because your name will be written there," and it was, "Oh God!" I'm squinting at these little nametags, thinking, ooh, that looks a little bit like it. I found it, but even when I found it I wasn't really sure. I kept looking at it going, "I think that's it".' She laughed raucously at her uncertainty and embarrassment. 'I wasn't really sure – and it's my own name!'

'It's my fault,' said Ching-Lee. 'I didn't teach my children Chinese. But by the time they went to school I thought I'd probably made a mistake and started to try and reverse the situation by taking them to Chinese classes. It didn't work because I was quite ambitious with the children: Cindy did ballet and they had swimming and they did violin. There were just too many extracurricular activities and something had to go and, unfortunately, we let the Chinese go. She speaks a bit of

Chinese. Her father and I would sometimes speak it around the house. We have relatives who speak it and, of course, the children picked up some. But it was funny, usually the minute her father and I decided to just speak Chinese in the house, Cindy and her brother would stand up and leave the room. They didn't want to know.'

'It would be nice to be able to speak Chinese,' Cindy said. 'But I certainly don't resent my parents making that decision because they didn't do it maliciously. They just thought it was the best decision at the time. I've had people come up to me saying, "Your parents; why didn't they get you to speak Chinese? That's a sin! What a shame! You poor thing. You must feel terrible that you can't speak Chinese." It's as if your parents robbed you of this really precious gift. So in a way, because of other people's reactions, I've actually gone the other way and said, "Well, look, it's just fine. They thought it was the right thing to do." And I think, as it turns out, yeah, it *is* a pity. But I certainly don't feel badly towards them for that. That's the least of a child's worries. If you're going to start resenting things like that, where are you going to stop?

'By the same token, since I've left home it's not like I've been prevented from going and learning Chinese. I have actually tried to learn a couple of times but I just never really prioritised it enough. So I'd do the first term or the first two terms and drop out because I was busy. I was always doing it after work and then I'd be doing something else and then it would interfere with something.'

191

The predicament of looking like a Chinese person but not speaking Chinese – what Cindy called not being 'a proper Chinese person' – was about to become acute. Cindy was going to travel to China for the first time in her life and find out in a very personal way what indeed it was to be a proper Chinese person. At her side would be her mother, Ching-Lee, who may have lost her language, but certainly not her memories of home.

In fifty years, Ching-Lee had been back to China only once. That had been a fairly recent occurrence, and then only with a stringently organised tour she'd taken with the members of her Saturday Chinese language class. It had left her no room to visit the sights of her childhood China which she had left behind when she was eight. Politics, mostly, had prevented Ching-Lee from going back. Politics and fear.

It was for these same reasons that Cindy had never been to China: politics and her parents' fear. In any case, her work commitments usually prevented her from much travel of any description. Still, she had occasionally entertained thoughts of going to China.

'Over the last few years, every time I've thought I might go to China, my mum's gone, "Oh no, don't go now. It's too dangerous." Or she would say, "You can fly to China but how are you going to travel *in* China? All the domestic planes go down; they crash",' Cindy laughed.

'Well, they used to go down a lot,' protested Ching-Lee.

'Originally my dad was really keen for me to go,' continued Cindy. 'If I said I was going anywhere else he'd say, "No, you shouldn't go there. You should go to China." Mum was the one always saying, "Oh, don't go, it's too dangerous. You won't be able to get out." And then, because I was in a mini-series about Tiananmen Square,' – Cindy played a feisty student leader in the mini-series which focused on the 1989 demonstration by a million pro-democracy students who were eventually moved by military force, resulting in countless deaths – 'Dad started saying, "Don't go. They'll recognise you and put you in jail." Stuff like that. Basically, we're a family of optimists,' Cindy deadpanned.

Ching-Lee had always wanted her children to go to China, eventually. 'I wanted them to go to instil some Chinese pride; to see that the Chinese people built the Great Wall, for instance. Many people might think that's a stupid thing to do but the fact that they did it is a wonder.'

But some of the fears she had had about going to China were based on firm realities. 'In the beginning we were worried about going back to China,' explained Ching-Lee, 'because China had the policy in the olden days that your face was your passport; in other words, if you had a Chinese face, they could claim you any time and there would be no way the Australian government could protect you. They could do that to you even though you might have been travelling under an Australian passport. But now China has taken that rule away. Now you are not a Chinese citizen unless you actually apply to be a Chinese citizen, because they've realised now that the one thing they've got enough of is people. They don't want any more. They'd rather you come back to visit and bring your money. There is a special term for Chinese returning to China. We are called "returned Chinese". They don't even recognise you as Chinese. You are a "returned Chinese". A *hwa chiao*. And they like *hwa chiaos* because they see them as having money. We don't all have money, but of course, compared to them we have money and so we are very welcome.'

By the time they were preparing to leave for China, Ching-Lee's fears were overcome by her excitement. Nothing would stand in her way. And for Cindy, well, the timing just seemed right.

'Going to China seemed like an important thing to do,' said Cindy. 'But it was never urgent so there was never any sense of timing, no sense of when to do it. None of that: "I have to go now" stuff. Also, I've never been a big traveller. But when I heard about the idea of going on the trip and taking a parent, it sounded really exciting. Not only would it be fun, it would be something I'd get a lot out of.'

Ching-Lee had embraced the idea, too. Not only did this trip present an opportunity to embark on a more personal journey to China, it meant spending time with her daughter.

'Mum's really excited to be going,' Cindy said before taking off. 'We're both excited. We usually have a really good time together. We're really close. I mean, we might have a fight,' she laughed, 'but it wouldn't be that bad a one.'

'I might have been worried that she might say the wrong thing,' Ching-Lee said quite seriously, then laughed at Cindy's look of mock offence. 'But I'm not apprehensive. I am still worried that in China people don't like to be criticised, especially about their political viewpoints. I would be worried if Cindy said the wrong thing there. But fortunately she doesn't speak Chinese.'

Ching-Lee could joke about it, but Cindy's only real apprehension about the trip was the language barrier. And it wasn't just that she might not be able to communicate, but that she might be judged for it.

'My friend, who's Chinese, can speak Chinese but her reading's not good,' said Cindy. 'When she's gone to China she says they reckon she's bunging it on; pretending she can't read when she really can. But she really can't.'

So how would they judge Cindy who could barely string two Chinese words together?

Language barrier aside, Cindy's expectations of her country of origin and what she'd find there weren't too high; rather, as always, her hopes were tempered with the strangely jolly, eccentric pessimism of the Pans. She was looking forward to seeing China and meeting her relatives, but philosophical about the realities and the possibility of disappointment.

'The whole thing about going to your motherland, and seeing your relatives, when you first think about it, it seems all really golden and you imagine you'll be leaping around in a field and really happy, and meeting your relatives will be like a Telstra ad, but it might not really be like that. My mum's relatives say they're really looking forward to seeing us, but you just don't know how people will feel on the day,' Cindy said.

'Your initial expectations are really high, but then you realise it might not be like that. Or even, I know people who really don't like China, don't like the people, don't like the country, and you know, maybe I won't like it and if I don't like it I don't think I'll feel very comfortable saying that. A lot of people in China are dying to get out. Heaps come out of China and don't want to go back. That's not a good sign.'

Cindy was also cautious in her expectations of what the experience might show her about herself and her Chineseness. 'I think it's possible that I'll come back changed,' she said. 'I don't know how, though. The only reason I think I could come back changed is because I hear other people saying it and I think, well, maybe that'll happen to me. But I am open to it. I am very open to it.'

Cindy and Ching-Lee would be going to Beijing, the great northern capital of the world's most populated country. From there, they would travel to the historically colourful, re-emerging financial centre of Shanghai, where Ching-Lee had spent those first years of her childhood.

Cindy was aware these were two burgeoning, buzzing

East meets West in Beijing

metropolises. But the vividness of the China of her imaginings came from stories of a pre-Cultural Revolution China.

'When I think of my parents growing up I always think of it as being really primitive,' she said. 'They had dirt floors and cooked over a wood stove. So for me there are two Chinas. One is what you see in the brochures and things, and in movies like *The Last Emperor* where it's all lavish. And then there's the China from what my parents have described to me, where everyone's really poor and wearing rags, this very peasanty existence, working their fingers to the bone; that kind of thing. My mum, apparently she was really skinny, begging for more food like Oliver Twist,' Cindy laughed.

'I remember the Second World War,' said Ching-Lee. 'We had a very hard time when the Japanese came and occupied Shanghai. Life was very difficult. I was quite sickly because food became very scarce and the quality was not good. I remember when there was only flour and my grandmother making noodles for us. Life was very hard for everybody. It was very, very basic.'

The reality of the new Beijing, their first port of call, is an amalgam of all those fabled images. But it is also a modern city, in some ways more westernised than the west. In scale alone, it outdoes most big cities. From the vast concrete expanse of Tiananmen Square to the freeway flyovers that ribbon through the city in a tangle that makes Los Angeles traffic look tame, seething Beijing is a testimony to the new era of growth and change China is experiencing. Massive high-rise apartment towers and obelisks of glass and steel housing huge corporations exist cheek by jowl with ornate, serene temples and old cobbled alleyways. McDonald's restaurants sit next to teahouses, businessmen with laptops and mobile phones walk by men with birdcages in their hands and pipes in their mouths. Old-fashioned markets trade side by side with high-gloss department stores. But all pervading is the constant presence of the Chinese military and the khaki, red and yellow images and symbols of Chairman Mao and his Cultural Revolution, still standing firm in the face of the new wave of capitalism.

Though a different reality from the stories of her childhood, Cindy liked Beijing from the minute she arrived. She liked its complexity – that it was not one thing or another, but a rich tapestry of its long history. So was this what it was to be properly Chinese? To be a mix of the old, the new and something altogether individual as well? It was early days, but Cindy felt optimistic that this enigmatic city held an answer to her question.

Another reality differed from Cindy's childhood fantasy: she was in a place where ostensibly she thought she would blend in. Yet she still felt different on many levels and this realisation opened her mind up to a new understanding of what it might mean to be Chinese.

Of course Cindy knew the old line 'all Chinese look the same' was a fallacy. But in Beijing she could see first-hand how wrong it was. 'I didn't see anyone who looked like me,' she said. 'I didn't see anyone who looked like Mum. I might have seen someone who looked a bit like my brother, but not really.'

Also Cindy's ancestry had always been somewhat puzzling to other Chinese people who had only her face to go on. The large, soft roundness of her eyes meant she was often mistaken for Japanese.

Lining up outside one of the Tiananmen Square monuments, Ching-Lee noticed two guards deep in discussion, all the while looking at Cindy and gesturing towards her. 'I could have sworn that the two guards were betting that Cindy was Japanese. Then they actually came up and asked me and I said, "No, she is Chinese".'

'Another time,' Cindy added, 'these other Chinese soldiers said to me, "Where are you from?" And they're dressed in uniforms and had guns in holsters and all those things, but they weren't unfriendly at all. I knew it wasn't an official thing and I knew what they had said so I wanted to use some of my Chinese on them. I said something that I thought meant "I'm from Australia". I said it very loudly and confidently and everyone turned around and looked at me and after a bit, Mum said, "You just said, 'Where is Australia?'"' Cindy exploded in laughter at the memory. 'Well, they just looked at me as if I was nuts and kind of walked off.'

But then, there were others who picked her as Chinese immediately.

'I knew that when they looked at me they knew I was Chinese, and they smiled at me,' she said. 'It felt like they were friendly and welcoming. That's why I felt sad that I didn't speak Chinese because a lot of people would come and talk to me, and I knew they were being friendly and might be saying interesting things, but I didn't really know what they were saying. Sometimes I could work out a little bit of what they were saying, but not often and that was a pity. What I felt lacking in myself was the language thing. Sometimes I started a conversation and it was an opening that I couldn't really take anywhere. I would have liked to talk to these people. This elderly gentleman said, "Sit down," in Chinese; I knew that much. And I thought, I would like to sit down but I can't talk to you. If I could talk to you I would sit down and have a bit of a chat, because he seemed like a really nice fellow. But I couldn't, so I didn't.

'Without the language you feel a bit miserable. It's like being a baby again, relying on someone else to sort it out all the time. And when you're used to being an adult and looking after yourself for so long, going back to that is very disempowering. Fortunately Mum was there, but even still it was a retrograde step for me having to ask my mum again, "Can you get me this?" "Can you get me that?" I hadn't done that for more than a decade.'

'Once, when we were ordering food,' laughed Cindy, 'I said what I thought was, "I don't understand," in Chinese. And then Mum said, "You just said, 'I'm not listening'!"'

'I admire her for trying,' laughed Ching-Lee. 'But Chinese is not easy.'

'Whatever I said,' added Cindy, 'I said it with confidence.' And mother and daughter laughed raucously.

Though Cindy felt alienated by her inability to communicate, she was noticing that being Chinese, even in China itself, meant so many different things. From the fancy, fashionable hairdressers in the old French Concession area to the soldiers in their pristine uniforms, and from the traditionally garbed old ladies to funky young girls; they were all proper Chinese people. Maybe she was, too.

'Across the board they were friendly and welcoming,' Cindy said, 'and that made me feel like I fitted in. Not to say I felt homogenous with the rest of the people, but I felt like I fitted in because I felt welcome as an individual.'

Walking through a colourful, chaotic market in Beijing, Cindy embraced the familiarity of the icons and trinkets sold there. They were as much a part of Australian–Chinese life as they were a part of life in China, and Cindy

Cindy leads the way at a Beijing market

told Eden stories about them. Eden was surprised at this person who claimed not to be a proper Chinese person and yet spoke like a walking encyclopaedia on China and its mythology.

'What I was saying about all those things might not have been, strictly speaking, absolutely correct, but it's correct as far as that's what I was told,' she laughed. 'But Eden asked me if my knowledge surprised me and it may have seemed I was being obtuse not saying, "Yes, I was surprised that I knew." But to me, it was like, "Well, I *am* Chinese. I do have Chinese parents. Of course I'm going to know this stuff." I knew it from my parents telling me stories and from various cultural activities I've been involved in, like being the Ambassador for Chinese New Year. That's caused me to do a lot of research and delving. And a lot of dancing things I'd done had exposed me to Chinese stories, such as the ballet of the Monkey King. I'd also performed in lots of plays and read different kinds of American–Chinese literature and seen Chinese films. So, you know, I'm definitely not any kind of authority on things but I guess I know quite a bit about China compared to a non-Chinese person.'

The welcome and enthusiasm that Cindy had felt was tempered with feelings of vulnerability, not just because she couldn't speak or understand the language, but also because of the way Chinese history was so sharply reflected in the present. While things were more relaxed in China just over a decade on from Tiananmen Square, the military presence in the streets was a bleak reminder of harsher times. You couldn't help wondering, especially if you were a foreigner with little or no knowledge of the Chinese language, what would happen if you were to find yourself in trouble in China.

One of the times when Cindy and Ching-Lee felt this most acutely was on their visit to the Chairman Mao Memorial Hall, the mausoleum on Tiananmen Square where the body of Mao Zedong is interred in a crystalline coffin. The coffin is raised from an earthquake-proof freezer, deep below the square, by elevator each morning, into a room where tourists and loyalists flow through nonstop every day. An intensely sombre place, the rules of conduct and security surrounding it are extremely strict. The atmosphere invoked Ching-Lee's old fears about travelling in China. And for once, Cindy understood fully that maybe her mother hadn't just been paranoid all those times she'd warned Cindy off visiting China.

'It was just the kind of strictness and the stringency of the rules and people kind of pointing at you and yelling at you and ordering you out of the line; you were sort of running around and feeling hassled,' Cindy said. 'You had to stay right in your line and not step out and we didn't read the sign that said you weren't allowed to carry any handbags, or even a plastic water bottle or camera. Nothing, basically. So we queued for what felt like an hour or something, got nearly to the front of the queue where you can actually enter the premises, because all the other queuing is right around the block, and they were pointing and yelling – and when you don't understand the language it seems a bit more harsh – ordering us out of the queue. A man escorted me to deposit our bags in this cloakroom-type thing but it wasn't the usual kind of cloakroom. Everyone was yelling and clamouring and barking and it was kind of scary. So basically we tried to go to the mausoleum three times before we actually got in. The first time, it was closed for renovations and the second time we had that problem with the bags and then when we tried to get back in the queue we couldn't get back in, and then the third time we of course didn't take any bags or anything but still didn't know what to expect. You stand in that queue and you can't talk and you feel like you can't make any sort of facial expressions, can't move your eye-balls or anything, and you have to take your hat off when you get inside. You felt that if you got in trouble – and those feelings are obviously quite exaggerated – they wouldn't throw you in prison or anything, but you feel intimidated and apprehensive and we had a lot of adrenalin coursing through our veins. Yet what we were doing was essentially a tourist activity.

'But it was a very exciting experience because I guess that feeling of, kind of being afraid basically, it was a bit foreign, really. And put it this way: when we got out at the other end I just felt so victorious. I felt like, wow, we did it. It was exciting because to see Chairman Mao in the flesh, that's pretty good,' Cindy couldn't resist a joke. 'If we'd gone there when he was alive we wouldn't have seen him in the flesh. And also because he dominated such a big important part of Chinese history. When I was growing up I remember hearing a lot about Chairman Mao, seeing pictures and that sort of thing so that sort of very much represents China for me.

'He didn't have a lot to say,' she added. 'But people were still buying plastic flowers for him.'

'Bigger than Mickey Mouse,' said Ching-Lee in that trademark deadpan, making both mother and daughter laugh raucously again.

The eyes in the giant portrait of Chairman Mao on Tiananmen Square follow you everywhere – except into the Imperial Palace, or the Forbidden City, as it was once known. This was the heart of old imperial China, where twenty-four emperors of the Ming and Qing dynasties had lived in excess and ruled with absolute power.

Eight hundred buildings of old Chinese elegance set on 720,000 square metres of ground make up the Forbidden City, each as beautiful as the next. 'This was originally built in the 1400s,' Cindy told Eden as they strolled across the complex. Towering temples and vast walls made them feel small and humbled. Huge carved lions, ceremonial rooms with gold leafing everywhere and long, labyrinthine hallways powerfully evoked the Manchus. 'To think that six hundred years ago people were living like this, and I mean when people talk about living like kings, this must be what they're talking about. It's so huge. Each of the palaces here is like a little palace and yet there are about ten of them.'

Eden asked Cindy if being there made her feel a sense of pride in coming from a culture that built such amazing structures.

'Well, proud; I guess so. Not that I had anything to do with it,' she laughed. 'But just as a human being, to know that human beings were doing this that long ago, that's fantastic.'

It was a telling answer. Even though she had only been in China a short time, Cindy was affirming something she perhaps had known all along: that though national-ity was important to identity, she valued individuality and humanity above it. Chairman Mao might have said that did not make her a proper Chinese person – he believed that individuality should be subsumed by one's duty to the state – but for Cindy, her exploration of her

Chinese heritage was strengthening her sense of self and her personal values.

'There was reinforcement of a sense of who I was,' she said, 'and feeling comfortable with being that individual person and not feeling like I'm a Chinese or I'm an Australian but that I'm an individual. I am who I am.'

And then to her delight Cindy discovered that her sense of individuality was perhaps a very Chinese thing. Before leaving for China, friends had told her about the morning rituals in Beijing parks where people gathered for their constitutionals. Cindy wanted to see the Chinese at leisure for herself and set out early to explore.

'I got to the park and I could just hear the music. I was trying to work out where it was coming from. Then I could see some people across a fence but I didn't know how to get to them. I had to ask people how to get there. Then when I got to them and saw all the people dancing, I must say for a while I just stood there and I felt tears coming. I felt so moved by that.'

As a wobbly, Chinese-instrumental recording of Engelbert's 'The Last Waltz' played from a tinny amplifier, Beijing dwellers paired up and danced in the old-fashioned way. It was non-competitive and had nothing to do with courtship. It was just dancing because it felt good, and the participants smiled serenely, away from their workdays in the concrete jungle or in sterile factories. They were at play and at peace amid greenery and nature.

The dancer in Cindy just couldn't stand by and watch and was delighted when she was invited to join in. She was partnered by an old but fit Chinese man, his long,

Transcending the language barrier in a Beijing park

wavy silver hair brushed back elegantly. Cindy could not speak to him much, nor he to her, but the dance transcended the language barrier and they smiled together, floating through the peace created by so many human souls collectively expressing their happiness in this most ancient of ways.

Talking about it later reduced her to tears of joy. 'This was so beautiful. A really beautiful thing,' she said. 'I think it is how people should be together: so many people harmonious and just enjoying themselves and everyone dancing to the same music, everyone doing their own patterns and no one interfering with each other. It was basically free and even just to watch, it was beautiful. It made me cry.

'That man came and asked me to dance and I felt really happy because I thought, I'm part of it, too. Also I felt like even though I couldn't speak Chinese, it didn't matter because we were dancing and we didn't have to talk. People were really nice to me and it just really felt like that was the way the world should be and I was part of it. It made me very happy.

'I thought that I would long remember that about China, maybe remember it above everything else, because I don't think I've experienced that, even in Australia. Dancing has always been really important to me but in Australia it's much more of a regimented thing. If you're dancing professionally, it's all about a hierarchy of standards. You want to be really good and when you take dancing class you're working and always thinking you're not good enough. You're not necessarily enjoying it and even if you are enjoying it, you're conscious of not being good enough. And then dancing socially in Australia it's always in these dirty nightclubs and there's all this smoke and it's really late at night and people are drinking and it's all sweaty and people are bumping you. Whereas here, even though it was so crowded, no one was bumping anyone. And it was bright and early in the morning. The air was so fresh. It was beautiful. That's the way it should be.

'We'd visited a temple in Beijing, a heavenly place. But dancing in the park, I thought, this is more like heaven to me. All these people moving harmoniously, so close together, no aggro, just so peaceful. When nine o'clock comes they go to their factory jobs, cleaning bottles or putting things in cartons. But they have this other life that's bright and clean. They're not getting anything out of the dancing other than they enjoy it.

'People say the way angels move is that they dance. I think us humans are always busy doing this and doing that, but if we don't have anything to do, why shouldn't we dance? Why shouldn't we just have that as a way to express our joy at being alive? That's beautiful. What would be better than that?'

On the trip out of Beijing they passed through rural beauty – forests and rivers, and men driving herds of goats along by hand or riding horses along the road. 'It made me aware of another face of China,' said Cindy. 'This lovely countryside was not something I usually associated with China.'

Cindy's spirit was still soaring when they made their way to the Great Wall of China. They visited a part of the Wall that was less frequented by tourists, and Ching-Lee, Cindy and Eden had the panorama virtually to themselves. Ching-Lee went to the Great Wall on her last trip but, because of her arthritic knees, had not made it to the top. Since then, she'd had surgery. And this time, by hook or by crook, she was going to make it. But how? Just then, a hawker came by with a small horse, offering it for rides up the rise. They all looked at each other. 'Okay,' pronounced Ching-Lee, though she was far from an equestrian. She *was* a good negotiator however, and after wearing the hawker down to an acceptable price, the horse was her steed. Next problem: how to get Ching-Lee up on it? Amid much laughter, modesty was put aside as they helped hoist Ching-Lee up onto her horse. Cindy and Eden took the steep climb by foot, only to get there, panting and exhausted. 'Giddy up, horsey!' Cindy greeted her mum. 'What took you so long?' Ching-Lee replied.

The last leg of the trip was up steep stairs to a watch tower perched on an undulant rise. Ching-Lee had to take it by foot. She had to stop and sit sometimes, but she made it, and she smiled and laughed victoriously as Cindy cheered proudly.

Giddy up, horsey! Ching-Lee prepares to take on the Wall

Once they reached the pinnacle, Cindy discovered another unexpected beauty, and this one took her breath away. 'In some ways I felt proud. This is in China. This is where I'm from. It was beautiful. But it wasn't so much about being Chinese,' she said. 'It was about thinking, wow, in the world there is this wonderful place. You really felt like you were sitting on top of the world. There was something about being able to see such a wide vista, and the way it was laid out made you feel as if you could see the curve of the world. And just the way the sun was and the sky that day, you felt, you know, you were near the roof of the world. It was very uplifting. A lot of natural settings can give you that sensation. But what was so impressive was not just the natural, but also the fact that this was a man-made structure and that it had been there for so many years.

'Also, it was part of my kind of bank of mythology. It was like when you see something that you have envisaged in a dream. The whole of China was really like that for me. Even though I'd never been there physically, it was something I'd been thinking about, hearing about and wondering about. I had so many pictures in my mind from looking at *China Pictorial*s and watching documentaries and obviously films and books and some of the acting things I'd done where I'd played this person from China. I had manufactured all these images in my mind which were very strong but based on pictures and photos and things like that. So seeing it in real life it was like, "Wow, you're walking around in your dream".'

Sitting on top of the world. Cindy with Eden at the Great Wall of China

Ching-Lee had another bank of images and though hers were based in reality, it was a long-ago reality, in pre-Communist Shanghai. Things had changed in Shanghai. The city had been left to decay for many decades during the Cultural Revolution, then in post-Mao China it had been regenerated to become one of the fastest growing cities in the world. When Ching-Lee lived there, the port city was the centre of European imperialism in China and a den of decadence, but she had known little of that. She just remembered, as a child, being taken care of by her grandmother and grandfather because her father was a diplomat and her parents were stationed overseas. They left Ching-Lee in Shanghai when she was ten months old because her father had been posted to Fiji and did not think that conditions there would be suitable for small children.

'As a young child, I never knew my parents. In fact, I often tell the story: I came home crying from school saying to my grandparents, "All the children out there are saying that you're not my mummy and not my daddy." And they said, "Well, of course we're not. Haven't you noticed you call us Grandpa and Grandma?" And I went, "Oh! Yes. So where is my daddy and mummy?" And they showed me pictures and said they were overseas. But I never knew what I'd missed. As far as I was concerned my grandma and grandpa were my parents. Our relationship was very good. I adored my grandmother.'

But Ching-Lee's parents had never intended to leave their babies – Ching-Lee and her older brother Ching-Tang – for so long. It was the Japanese invasion of China that had prevented them from coming back or from even providing support for their family during the extreme hardship of the occupation. Eight years later, at the end of World War Two, Ching-Lee's parents were finally able to go home. After a brief stint back in China, Ching-Lee's father was posted to Indonesia. While there, Sukarno became President and recognised the Communists as government in China. Since Ching-Lee's father was an appointee of the now banished Nationalist Government, he was forced to seek asylum elsewhere.

Ching-Lee's father had diplomat friends in Australia

as his first diplomatic posting had been to Melbourne, so he now chose that city as home for his family.

It was all so long ago but Ching-Lee vividly remembered the place where they had lived in Shanghai, right in the city centre. 'It was very simple. We were upstairs in a very big room. There were two double beds. I slept with my grandmother. There was a big table in the middle where we all ate together. And at the back there was a partitioned off area where the maid lived and where the cooking was done and the commodes were kept. I don't know whether I could find it again,' Ching-Lee said before the trip. 'And I believe they have changed all the street names now, so it would be hard to find.' The Communists had indeed changed street names during the Cultural Revolution, making the tracing of such memories all the more difficult for *hwa chiaos* like Ching-Lee returning after so many years.

But they were on their way to Shanghai to see what they could find, travelling by train from inland Beijing to the famous port which lay on the extreme of China's eastern bulge that extended into the North Pacific.

The train trip made Ching-Lee nervous. 'All those Japanese soldiers; I was terrified of them when I was little,' she explained. 'So the fact that there were soldiers every time we went anywhere in China was always scary for me. They've got guns. They can arrest you. Any time, they could turn nasty.'

Cindy added, 'For me, not speaking the language, you feel like they could carry you away and lock you up and you wouldn't be able to defend yourself.'

They never felt more vulnerable than on that train, when an official in a uniform marched up the carriage and demanded quietly but firmly that Ching-Lee follow her out of the compartment.

'Eden thought we must have been in trouble because David had been filming a little bit and we weren't sure if that was all right,' Ching-Lee said. 'So Eden gave me a little toy koala to give them as a sweetener. They said: "Why are you filming?" I just said, "Oh, my friends are interested in photography".'

And that, much to everyone's relief, was the end of it.

'Mum was very capable of wheeling and dealing,' said Cindy, with not a little admiration for her mother's cool head in the situation. 'Yeah, it was good. Nice change. I was shocked.' She laughed merrily, as did Ching-Lee – it was easy to see the funny side after the event.

But the train incident brought back memories for Ching-Lee of hearing first hand stories of the brutality of Mao's regime, of the threats of being taken away, and of relatives being forced to live their lives in accordance with the edicts of the state.

Many of Ching-Lee's relatives had been harshly affected by such policies. One of these was her cousin Shao-Yin, whose home would be their first stop in Shanghai.

For Cindy, this visit to Shao-Yin's was an opportunity to see old Shanghai. 'They lived in this little apartment in a sort of complex, but once you got inside the complex it was quite old-fashioned,' she said. 'The road was dirt and cobblestone, and the way it was laid out was pretty amorphous. We weren't sure we would be able to find it. It wasn't like there was a buzzer system and all that sort of thing. We had to leave the road and go down an alleyway.'

'Mind you,' added Ching-Lee, 'she doesn't have to live there. There are plenty of new apartment buildings but she wants to live in Shanghai itself. She's right in the middle of the city. She prefers to be in the city because she doesn't have a car and all the shops and conveniences are nearby. All her life she has lived there except when she was forced to move to the country during the Cultural Revolution. Because she was one of three children, one child had to go to the country and she, being the oldest at that time, that was how they decided she should go. She had a terrible time. That was really awful for her because she never really got a proper education. It was the youngest that got the education.'

Little wonder then that Shao-Yin now enjoyed living exactly where she felt like living.

As they neared Shao-Yin's apartment Cindy began to worry about what her reaction would be. Essentially, the only thing they had in common was blood. Was it thicker than water? 'With some relatives you don't really know,' said Cindy. 'There's a semi-presumption that they will be very welcoming and loving. But if you think about it, you're really strangers and some relatives can behave in a very unpredictable way. So you wonder what they're going to be like.'

When they arrived at Shao-Yin's, though, all her anxiety melted away. There was that simple connection of shared heritage. An intuitive knowing enveloped them as

Group hug – Shao-Yin embraces Cindy and Ching-Lee

soon as Shao-Yin, in the company of her younger sister, Shao-Ping, greeted Ching-Lee with hugs and laughter and huge, welcoming smiles. And as Shao-Yin hugged her mother, Cindy hugged the two of them, overjoyed by the moment. 'There was just so much warmth in that room. It was great,' she said. 'I felt a connection. Though we hardly knew each other, we weren't strangers at all. We had history and heritage. And that's a pretty strong bond.'

Throughout the afternoon, they looked at photo albums and traded stories, filling in the years and looking to the future.

'It makes me feel that I wish I had come back earlier,'

said Ching-Lee, simply. 'I could have made contact earlier and had a closer relationship, but I am glad I am here now.'

As for Cindy, did the meeting fulfil her expectations of leaping around in a field or being in a Telstra ad? 'I always think of those Telstra ads as featuring lots of pasta, tomatoes and Italians. So, no, not exactly,' she laughed. 'It was a different feeling. A very real, very personal one. It just felt good. I don't know how else to say it. They were certainly very welcoming and the whole thing was very warm and if there was a field nearby, well, I probably would have leapt around in it. I felt that happy.'

Since arriving in Shanghai, Ching-Lee had been haunted by vivid thoughts and memories of the woman from whom she had been separated by the tide of world events all those years ago: her grandmother. With its new office towers and hustle and bustle, this was not the Shanghai of her childhood, but the beautiful Art Deco buildings that had characterised the city since the twenties were still in abundance.

Inspired, Ching-Lee went in search of the home she had shared with her grandmother in those early years. She didn't think she had much of a chance of finding it after such a long time because the Communists had changed the street names and Shanghai's growth had squeezed out many of the old residential buildings. She didn't know that her memory would serve as a good compass.

Eden, Cindy and Ching-Lee found what Ching-Lee thought was her old street, which used to be called Seymour Road. She knew the street number of the building in which she'd lived, thirty-three, but she also knew that when her brother had once gone looking for the dwelling, he'd had no luck.

Here on this street Ching-Lee found a building at number thirty-three that looked very much like the home she had left when she was eight years old. Rundown and ramshackle, it was a dark apartment block of old Shanghai style. Beyond its arched doorway the foyer was filled with bicycles and dust, and an old cherrywood staircase led up to the residences.

Ching-Lee remembers her beloved grandmother in the stairwell of her old home

Ching-Lee stopped at the bottom of the staircase – if it was not the home of her childhood, she thought, then it was exactly the same style. Placing a foot on the very first step, her emotions overflowed. Fifty years of missing that beautiful woman who had nurtured her surged through Ching-Lee there on that stairway, and she wept. 'I miss my grandmother,' she said softly. Cindy stood silently by, giving her mother space to remember and to grieve.

In the gloomy upstairs, Ching-Lee found an apartment just like the one where she'd spent most of her first decade. In the hallway outside, Ching-Lee remembered there had been a bathtub. As she entered the big room, just like the room where they had eaten, slept, and shared their lives, for a moment she was a little girl again, just out of that tub, warm and safe and ready to share a meal at the large table that once dominated the space.

Narrating each turn through a doorway, each view out a window as if it were her own house, she showed Cindy and Eden through. 'If this is not it, then it is exactly the same,' she said and wept some more. It was a strange, ghostly homecoming, and as she sat down with the current resident of the apartment, Ching-Lee tried to put it into words. 'I have been very moved because of my grandmother. I feel very soft towards her. I wish I could see her again, to tell her how much I care about her. It's too late now, of course.' And she broke down again.

For Cindy it was an intimate view of her mother's past and her heritage. 'I come from very humble circumstances,' Ching-Lee said to her, knowing that being in this place made real the stories she had shared with her daughter. Cindy now not only had pictures, but the sensation of walking through the landscape in which her mother had grown up.

'A lot of the façades in Shanghai looked fairly modern,' Cindy said. 'There were banks and corporate headquarters. But if you went behind them you would find all these old places like this one. Walking down the street you could see down little alleyways and passageways, and even though the front looked quite modern and European, you could see people washing out of bowls and looking much more primitive.'

Moreover, she had seen how much her great-grandmother had meant to her mother. And she had glimpsed the little girl in her mother.

'Spending this time here has been a revelation for me, uncovering just a corner of my ancestry,' said Cindy. 'Maybe there's something that's always been here that's part of me. Maybe I shouldn't leave it behind.'

The images of her mother's early years were now so strong it seemed they would stay with her forever and remind her of the place from which her mother had come.

In nearby Suzhou, the original home of her ancestors, Cindy discovered another small, but significant detail that spoke to her Chinese identity. The trip was almost over and she had not yet had time to digest all she had seen in China, but there, at Suzhou railway station, a sweet, familiar smell seemed to give shape to her whole experience.

'When we got off the train, all these people were trying to sell us these little bunches or bracelets or hair bands made of Chinese magnolias. We had some of those trees at our house in Wahroonga and I remembered that really well. And also at the surgery where I work, the guy who owns it, his Chinese father is always bringing these flowers in. So it was like, "Oh! This really is a Chinese thing." Those sorts of details really tied things together for me. I guess in a way it gave it some validity for me.'

Whether in Australia, or in Beijing, these were things that proper Chinese people did.

On her last morning in China, Cindy returned to the park where she had danced and cried. Some people were doing Tai Chi, moving rhythmically and gently to wake up their bodies, while others were dancing with big red flags or fans. Many of them were still in their pyjamas. The sight filled Cindy with another rush of joy.

'It makes you think, what other things, if you were to live here, would you discover that would be really wonderful and lovely like this? It's so simple. All it is, is people and nature but really *in* nature and experiencing it genuinely every day. A lot of the face that China puts to the world is stern,' she said. 'You see the soldiers walking in this very regimented way at those parades, seeming stern-faced and conforming to some overriding direction. It makes you think you wouldn't like to live there. It is quite controlled and you can't be an individual. But then you come to the park and you realise there is this whole other side. Where else could you walk around in your pyjamas and do all kinds of funny movements, rub your tummy, rub your face, shake it all around? You can walk however you like, you can start dancing anywhere, even singing, and no one's going to bother you. No one minds. They're all watching you enjoy yourself. There's a real sense of freedom and this is maybe what they're really like. But sometimes when you see them walking down the street or at bus stations they look kind of stern, and you think it's grey and drab. But in the park, there's lots of colour, red fans, and all this greenery as well. The best part of it is, everyone's actually enjoying it. They come every day and do their exercises and walk around.

'Sometimes in Australia we think we're really free but if you start doing unusual things, people look at you and think you're weird. If you're walking in an unusual way in the city, people might think you're a psych patient. The Chinese don't seem vain about clothes. They don't seem to spend a lot of money on them. They tend to look more at your face, instead of checking out your clothes. In Australia, you check out the whole package. But looking at a person's face: that's more the essence of who they are. I think the parks in Beijing are great. Why shouldn't we walk around in our pyjamas?'

When she returned to Australia, Cindy didn't suddenly start walking around Sydney's Botanic Gardens in her pyjamas, but months later she was able to reflect on what her trip to China meant to her. It had given her a great gift: a real sense of peace about who she was.

'I feel more confident about being an individual,' she said. 'I didn't feel the same as all those people there. But in the way I don't feel I'm the same as everyone here in Australia, I don't feel that I'm the same as everyone there. Maybe when I was little I thought it would be nice to be in China and look the same as everyone else and be the same as everyone else. But now I'm thinking, maybe it wouldn't. Maybe I still wouldn't have looked the same. I was thinking, oh, won't it be interesting having everyone speaking Chinese and having everyone looking Chinese. But I don't think people *did* look like us. So you know what I mean? I didn't feel like I'd found a whole lot of people like me. And even if they had looked like me, they're not like me because they're not Australian born Chinese and they don't share just all the myriad of different things that make up what my identity is.

'But the trip made me think about it a bit more and I definitely feel like a real Chinese person. It made me feel that this idea of being a real Chinese person – well, anyone who has any claim to being Chinese *is* a real Chinese person. I am more comfortable with the fact that there's lots of different kinds of Chinese and even if other Chinese people don't realise you're Chinese, that doesn't mean you're not.

'When I was walking around in China, I didn't feel the same as all the people there, but that doesn't mean I'm not Chinese.

'I think the trip helped with that particular journey; you feel a bit more confident going, "Oh, that doesn't mean I'm like that. I'm me and it's okay." You don't have to restrict yourself because you're Chinese. Other people might pigeonhole you but you don't have to pigeonhole yourself.'

Ching-Lee's health has not been the greatest since the trip to China. Even so, she's still as quick to laugh as she ever was. She still smiles that great, full-faced grin that is the epitome of joy. And she and Cindy are still the banter twins, sending each other up lovingly. Ching-Lee puts on a very brave face. That's one thing that hardship in childhood teaches a person.

Even so, Ching-Lee readily admits: in the face of uncertain health she is very, very pleased that she went to China with Cindy when she did. 'We travelled to Paris together some years ago and that was wonderful. But I loved being in China with Cindy. It was very special, of course, because it is where we are from. It was the trip of a lifetime for that reason. And it was great to see it through her eyes, and for her to see it through my eyes. But the best thing was simply being there together. That was wonderful.'

Cindy concurred. 'Seeing my mum's home gave me a new sense of certainty about some things. And seeing her there gave me a new insight into her. And that's something I will always be grateful for.'

Cindy still thinks, every now and then, of dancing in that Beijing park, and of her lovely, graceful dancing partner there. And now, she also thinks about her relationship with China as a kind of dance. A dance with strangers but a dance they all know; an instinctive, soul-inspired dance to the rhythm of being Chinese.

'When I danced with the Ballet Ensemble, we would make up ballets. It was a group of musicians and dancers,' said Cindy. 'The musicians would compose and we would choreograph and put the whole thing together. It was great. We did some Asian-inspired stories, including *The Monkey King*. Even though I'd seen the TV show, *Monkey*, and knew the story, it wasn't like it meant much to me. I hadn't sat down and read it. I didn't really read Chinese fairytales. But to actually make up our own ballet about it brought it alive for me. I got more into the story and developed my own kind of attachment to it, and that made all the difference.

'The trip to China was like that for me. I had this kind of second-hand knowledge of it. But in going, I formed my own attachment; my own bank of experiences. I got to dance my own Chinese dance, you could say. It became personal – and it brought China alive for me. And it brought more to life the proper Chinese person in me.'

Those who cannot see where they came from . . .

Will never get to where they are going.

JOSÉ RIZAL

Craig Wing
Filipino Australian

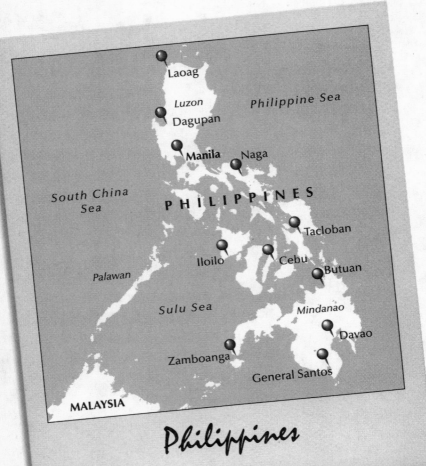

Laoag

Luzon

Philippine Sea

Dagupan

Manila Naga

*South China
Sea*

P H I L I P P I N E S

Tacloban

Iloilo Cebu Butuan

Palawan

Mindanao

Sulu Sea Davao

Zamboanga

General Santos

MALAYSIA

Philippines

Counting His Blessings

'I know nothing about my Filipino heritage, which is quite sad . . .

growing up in Australia I always considered myself Australian

and that was as far as it went.'

Craig Wing is one lucky boy. He is a star of Rugby
League, a naturally gifted sportsman, smart, and not bad
looking to boot. Growing up he was nurtured in every
way by devoted parents and lived in the sunny seaside
suburb of Maroubra in Sydney's southeast. Back in the
eighties, Maroubra wasn't as flash as it is today, but for
a sports-mad kid like Craig it was heaven: a rambling
mixture of ocean beach, acres of ovals and bushy public
space. And it seemed young Craig had kicked a ball over
the entire length and breadth of it.

His childhood was always sports-orientated. He'd

played football on the weekend for as long as he could remember. Since the age of five, he played Rugby Union and Rugby League every weekend. In summer it was athletics and cricket. His life was sport.

And so the writing was on the wall. Having grown up in an area crazy about its very own Rugby League team, the South Sydney Rabbitohs, it was only natural that a rising star like Craig would find his way into that team's ranks. He made his mark with his signature explosive speed in his home turf team, before settling into some serious consolidation with the prestigious Sydney Roosters as a star halfback, his talent and reputation growing exponentially with each game he plays.

He is also articulate. With a promising career in television as a roving reporter on the Foxtel cable TV network, even his future outside football looks assured. But without football or a TV career Craig Wing's talents would probably have seen him succeed anyway. He was a straight-A student at high school, and was the responsible type with obvious leadership qualities: he'd been class captain, captain of the cricket team, captain of the universe it seemed, during his school years. 'It was a small school,' he demurred and, of course, his natural humility just makes him all the more appealing. He is polite and charming, the sort of guy a girl could ecstatically take home to meet the parents.

In other words, he is almost too good to be true.

There is little doubt, however, that had Craig been born into his mother Editha's native city of Cebu in the Philippines, his chances of success would have been greatly diminished. Cebu is a place where the third world collides none-too-prettily with the first; where people battle to survive in third-world poverty and over-crowding in the midst of out-of-control first world urban development. In the Philippines Craig would simply not have had the opportunities he has enjoyed in Australia.

But Craig never really had cause to think about that. He'd been born in Australia and into a family which, though not wealthy by any means, was never left wanting for anything thanks to the hard work of both parents.

'I'm an Australian. I grew up in Australia. I've never considered myself anything else,' said Craig. And despite his exotic looks, he never had reason to think any differently. His parents certainly didn't give him reason to. They had not deliberately denied their children knowledge of their Asian heritage, it was just that they were busy getting on with the here and now and looking to the future for their kids. There wasn't a lot of space in their lives for history.

The Wings are a pretty solid bunch, the kind of mum-dad-and-the-kids you could put on a TV ad and sell an Australian audience just about anything. If there's any such thing as a typical twenty-first century Aussie family, then Craig Wing's family is it: a close-knit, rowdy mob bonded by do-anything-for-each-other loyalty and love. They are five kids and two dedicated parents who share deep mutual respect, a wicked sense of humour and a great propensity for ribbing each other mercilessly.

Without affectation or conceit themselves, the Wings also share a distrust of pretenders and snobs, as well as a strong work ethic that has been tirelessly instilled in them by the head of the family, Craig's dad, Allan. The abiding philosophy of this household has always been: do the right thing, put in the effort and get the most out of life.

Amid all that getting on with it, the Wing kids didn't have much time to get caught up in the issue of their ethnicity. And in any case it seemed there wasn't much to get caught up in. 'These days, I don't think anybody really gets picked on in relation to nationality, for not being Australian,' said Craig. 'It'd more likely be, for example, a person of Vietnamese origin telling a Lebanese person that Vietnamese was better or vice versa.'

Craig and his four sisters identified with mainstream Australian society; they did not segregate themselves or feel any need to develop a sense of belonging to the Philippines. They did not, for instance, learn their mother's language or Filipino traditional dance or belong to any Filipino cultural groups. Nor did their mother. None of the children ever really felt Filipino. In fact, the Wing kids were known to tease their mum, making fun of her English and the way she said things. 'They get a bit cranky at me because I have been here so long and my English is not so good,' said Editha, laughing. 'But it is all joking around.'

Born in 1979, Craig Wing began school when the face of Australian society was changing. The White Australia

Policy was well and truly gone and Asian faces of all kinds were becoming much more common in the school-yard. However, Craig's Eurasian looks weren't easy to categorise.

Craig remembered some schoolyard teasing because he looked *different*. 'I was quite dark as a child and there weren't too many dark kids around when I was at kindergarten, and I suppose I copped a little bit of teasing then. But it never really worried me. Dad always used to say that they were just jealous because I had a good tan,' he laughed. 'And I suppose in early high school no one could really tell what nationality I was. I got called everything from Aboriginal to wog to Asian. But that was just mucking around in high school. I never took it to heart. It's just the way guys in particular are: they'll find something and work at it and work at it and work at it . . .' he laughed again. 'But at school it was never an issue for me because I was always really good at sport. I was more a leader than a follower.'

'He could fight a bit, too,' said his dad, Allan. 'Craig was not just a good sportsman, but he was a fair player. He didn't cheat at anything. He played to the best of his ability and he had that discipline factor. Plus I used to say to him, "Don't ever start a fight, but don't let some bastard beat you if he does." He did some martial arts. I wanted him to be able to defend himself. If he was going to cop some crap for his ethnicity or whatever . . .'

'I wasn't one of these people who was an easy target,' said Craig. 'I might have copped a bit of flack and that was probably for my dark skin more than anything, but

I suppose with all of us, you couldn't really pick what we were.'

'All the girls at school were a bit keen on him,' added Allan. 'He was always a skinny little bugger but he was cute then. He was always good at his grades; always top of the class or near top. He was dux of the year at his primary school and got eleven out of twelve of the awards: all the cricket, football, the whole thing. He was right at the forefront and the teachers were all on side with him, and the other players all wanted him to play with them because he was a winner and gave everything to what he did. So he was very fortunate.'

None of the Wing kids ever really felt different from the Australian norm. Allan and Editha Wing tried to make sure of it, believing that a bright future was possible for all of their children so long as they nurtured in them an ability to get along with everybody and to look on everyone as equals. This ethos encompassed them all in every way, and none of the Wings was ever too old to be reminded of that. Regardless of Craig's fame all were equal and were expected to do their best with each of their God-given talents.

It's not surprising that the Wings didn't give much thought to keeping up their ties with Editha's large extended family in the Philippines – there had always been more than enough going on in their nuclear family to keep them all busy. From the time Craig had first showed his incredible sporting talent, aged around five, the Wings had been constantly on the go. Allan and Editha – who already had Annabelle, three years older than Craig – both worked shifts at Qantas, earning enough money to keep their boy in footy boots and Little Athletics gear, cricket whites and karate uniforms. More kids came along – Danielle, Taryn and Kirsty – and soon Allan was running Craig back and forth from his carnival of sporting activities, getting the girls to and from netball, and overseeing their homework, while Editha stoked the engine room, packing endless lunches and getting dinner on the table, before heading off for her early shift at the airport. As their children grew, the pace never seemed to slow; one of the girls, Danielle, was doing year twelve, another, Annabelle, was about to be married – it never stopped.

The Wings had been back to the Philippines to visit Editha's family once sixteen years before, when Craig was five going on six, his sister Annabelle was nine, and Danielle was only two. They'd spent a month there.

Editha Wing had gone back on her own once since then, but that was eleven years ago. 'I never had the time,' she said. 'All the time I was focused on my kids, making sure they were all right. I was always worried about their health or whether they were doing well at school. I didn't worry about myself. I just worried about them. They are my life. I was always busy so I didn't think of going back.'

But Eden Gaha was about to change that. Editha and Craig would go back to the Philippines with a little encouragement from Allan, allowing Eden to chronicle their journey in *The Ties That Bind* documentary. And Craig would come to see just how lucky he really was.

Before he was approached with the idea of going to the Philippines, Craig was named *Cleo* magazine's Bachelor of the Year. Craig had little time to reflect on his new status as the country's best catch though. Everything in Craig's life took second place to footy. He was too busy getting on with training and playing to bathe in any glory.

For Craig, the only thing that was more important than football was his family. His mother and father, and even his sisters who'd grown up watching him play endless matches, had always gone all-out to help him fulfil his dreams. 'When you see kids who have kicked on,' Allan said, 'I don't think a lot of them could have done it without their family and the sacrifices, really, both from themselves and from their families.' Craig never needed to be reminded of that, but he always seemed to have too little time to spend with those he loved.

With two training sessions a day, club-related pro-motional work and media commitments, top footballers like Craig don't get much time off. But he had always come home for dinner at least once a week and devoted the scant two weeks break he was given off at Christmas to hanging out with his family.

There was one great pleasure that Craig did take for just himself. In the month he got off between the end of the season and pre-season training, he liked to get out of Sydney and go travelling. Allan, who had backpacked all over the world as a young man, encouraged his son in this. 'When you're away from everything you know, you've got to be responsible,' Allan said. 'You've got to be responsible for your own health, for your financial situation, et cetera. And it makes you appreciate life. When you come from a country where you've got everything, and go to a country where they haven't, it makes you grow up.'

However, when Eden first approached Craig about going to the Philippines to shoot the documentary during that precious break, Craig wasn't immediately keen. Going to the Philippines was not something that had crossed his mind. He had so little time off and in that time he liked to indulge his passion for new places. He'd been to the Philippines before, albeit when he was six. 'I like to try and go somewhere different each time,' he said. But the truth was that he was a little nervous about confronting this largely unknown side of his family.

Plus, the Wings were pretty humble people, so the idea that Craig and Editha would be making an episode for a television documentary was not one that was met with their unbridled enthusiasm.

'I am always proud of my kids,' laughed Editha. 'But I don't go around bragging about them.' At first she saw getting involved in the documentary as tantamount to showing off. Craig wasn't sure he wanted to put his family in the spotlight either, especially if his mum didn't feel comfortable.

'We're not braggers or big heads or blow-hards or show-offs,' said Allan. 'If I saw any of those traits coming out in the kids, they'd wear a size eight and a half up the rear end. I don't think there's any room for that. And my wife is a little bit shy. She doesn't tell anybody who her son is.'

Indeed, Editha hadn't even made a big deal of Craig's success to her own family in the Philippines. 'I don't want them to think my attitude has changed. I don't want them to think of me as considering myself above anyone. So I don't really talk about it.'

But Allan saw Eden's offer as a great opportunity for Craig and Editha to share an important experience together, and he talked them around to the idea. 'Dad always convinces me to do things,' said Craig, smiling.

Craig's concerns about the trip went much deeper than the worry of being seen as a show-off, though. 'My reticence, I suppose, was because of the confrontational aspect to it. A lot of people tend to steer clear of confrontation. And the documentary would be showing the public a side to me that they might not have thought existed. Especially me living the way I do now, doing the things I'm doing, the lifestyle I'm living, people might not expect the humble circumstance of my mother's people. My natural instinct was to go, "Nah, I could do something else." But Dad always puts things into perspective with the merits of this and that.'

'I told them it's a great opportunity,' said Allan, 'and a great honour to be chosen. Out of all the Filipinos in Australia, you're the ones. My wife was a bit worried. There was a lot of built-up emotion for her. We are a complicated mixture in many ways. But we loved the Philippines and in the end, she thought it would be a good thing not only for her and Craig, but for her family and, in a small way, for the Philippines.'

'When I first thought about it, I was ambivalent,' said Craig. 'But I began to realise that it was a chance to do something different, see something different and to go with my mum. When I really thought about it, I realised it was something that, if given the opportunity, I had to do if for no other reason than for my mum. She's always felt very close to her family and has always believed that the children are the ones to take care of the parents when they're older, and I think she feels a bit detached from that living here and not being able to see them. And she doesn't really talk to them too often on the phone. But she still feels close to them. I felt it would be really good for her to see how her family was, especially her parents.'

And Allan thought it might be good for Editha to maybe take some credit where credit was due. She'd brought up a great son. She deserved to show him off.

Over the years, Allan Wing's love of travel and his desire to educate his kids in the ways of the world so that they might appreciate what they had, saw the family travel to Bali, Thailand and the Philippines together. 'My dad was never one to do what the tourists do,' said Craig. 'When we went away we always stayed in decent hotels but we didn't really eat in restaurants. We ate how the locals ate in little stalls off the side of the street. He wanted us to see how people in third world countries live. It was very much an eye-opener, seeing people content with living with so little. It made us see that the material possessions that we worried about so much really weren't that important.'

But now it was a different world. Craig's in particular. 'He's been given opportunities that he's got to take now. He can't just put things on hold for travel, especially the kind I did, sleeping on beaches in a sleeping bag, living on food from street vendors,' Allan said.

'I don't have much time and if I'm going to travel, I'm going to enjoy it,' said Craig. 'And it's true that there's a lot of things I can't do. But I'm doing things that most people don't dream about.'

This trip to the Philippines, however, would be a different kind of travel entirely. It would mean so much more to Craig than a break away from Sydney and his gruelling schedule.

'I know nothing about my Filipino heritage,' Craig said on the eve of leaving for Manila, 'which is quite sad. Growing up, Mum never taught us any Tagalog, or Visayan which is the dialect she knows. I suppose it might have been good to know another language, but I think growing up in Australia I always considered myself Australian and that was as far as it went.'

Now he felt that he should know more about that heritage and the members of his extended Filipino family. But, most importantly, he knew this trip was going to be a very emotional journey for his mum and he was glad he would be there to share it with her.

For Editha, the reality of the trip was just sinking in. 'All my brothers and sisters live in different places now,' she said. 'I have one sister in Germany, two brothers living in Australia, a sister in Spain. Only one brother lives with my parents, and another in the same city.' Then the emotion caught up with her. 'I don't know how we're going to be,' she said and suddenly began to weep, 'because it's been a long time. They will probably be happy to see me. But I don't know what they're going to look like. Maybe my mum and dad will be looking old. I'm not sure if they're healthy. And Mum's place may not be one hundred per cent because the children aren't there to look after the place. There's not much help looking after it. I don't know. It's been eleven years.

'I miss them a lot. Especially my dad. I heard that he is not feeling well. So this time, going back, I am really looking forward to it because who knows how long they are going to be around? Last night I started to cry because I just can't believe I am going back. And I am hoping that they are all right. I can't wait to see them now.'

Manila is not the world's favourite destination. Allan loved the Philippines' capital; it appealed to the traveller in him, his love of the exotic, his interest in the third world. Still, his time there he remembered as hard. 'I was coming from a society where you knew things worked and there was organisation, to a place where there just wasn't,' he explained. 'And you could see all these old buildings just being allowed to crumble and everything was decrepit. There were horses in all the streets. I don't mind that sort of thing. That's the attraction . . . but when you're living there for twelve months and the tropical weather is relentless and you're stepping through manure and puddles and there are no manhole covers, your nerves get frayed.'

Editha agreed: 'It would pour rain, all day, all night, all week. The ground was all mud and holes.'

As she and Craig boarded their flight for Manila, Editha's expectations of what she'd see in that city weren't high; she didn't imagine much would have changed. Manila might have been only half a day's plane trip away, but it was a whole other world.

When they landed, Editha's expectations were pretty much confirmed. 'There were just twice as many people,' she said. 'It wasn't raining at least. It was nice and sunny.'

But sun or no sun, Craig hated it at first sight. Not an auspicious start to the trip. 'He thought there were too many people. It was too crowded. Very dirty,' Editha said.

'I couldn't stand it,' said Craig. 'It was just too densely populated and you felt like you couldn't breathe. I really didn't think it would get to me so much. The congestion and so much going on twenty-four hours a day and people living on top of each other. It really made me look at where I live in Sydney and appreciate it so much more. And to also realise, you've got to expect that sort of hustle and bustle when you go to an Asian city.'

'Luckily, we didn't stay in Manila,' said Editha. Instead, they used it as a base to travel to other parts of the nation of islands. 'Out there, everyone was relaxed, not rushing like in the city. The locals would just sit in their front yards watching the world go by. It was peaceful, cool, nice to get out of Manila. Once you get out, everything is much prettier, much more peaceful.'

On their first trip out of Manila they drove to the town of Pagsanjan. From there they took a two-hour trip to Pagsanjan Falls, ferried by two skilful boatmen who worked in tandem to manoeuvre the canoe upriver against a mighty current. In a boat with his mum, Craig could forget about the stress of Manila and just enjoy her company. 'Seeing her on her own turf being a Filipino, I'm seeing a totally different side to her. It's really good, just hanging out. She's relaxed and not distracted and we can really talk. I guess that's because I'm relaxed and not distracted by other things either.'

Craig already related well to his mum. 'As you get older I guess you appreciate your parents more.' But being able to hang out with her like a friend was an experience he found very special. 'Just the simple fact of being able to spend time, one-on-one with my mum like that, I don't think I'd ever done it before.'

'All the time in the Philippines people were saying we were brother and sister, we got on so well,' smiled Editha. 'It was really great having that time to spend together.'

She and Craig fell into a playful mode, laughing and joking with each other, Editha gently pinching Craig on the arm at a cheeky comment, Craig casually throwing his arm around Editha's neck like one buddy to another. For Craig, sharing this with his mum reaffirmed their closeness. 'We're great mates,' he said. 'And it's fantastic to have that sort of relationship with your mum.'

They swam at the falls and then, after an exhilarating ride along the rapids, they set out to visit the home of Editha's brother Reuben. Editha wasn't expecting Reuben to be there – he was a merchant seaman and she assumed he was still at sea – but she was really looking forward to catching up with his family.

Craig and Editha take on the rapids at Pagsanjan Falls

It was on the way to Reuben's tiny town outside Batangas that Craig began to learn more of his mother's history. There were none of the distractions they both had back in Sydney: footy practice, meals to be prepared; Craig's busy schedule that often saw him fly out the door straight after a home-cooked meal and Editha's attention split five ways among all her children. Editha began to reveal how it was she'd left Cebu for her new life in Australia.

Allan and Editha Wing's union was the kind of serendipity that might have made even sceptics wonder about the part that destiny plays in life. It was the 1970s, and Allan was doing the young Australian thing: he was on a backpacking odyssey that had taken him through Europe, then through Asia. When he arrived in the Philippines, Allan's plan was to stay there for the two-month extent of his visa, then wrangle a cheap airline ticket for the United States via Bangkok.

But in his first week in the Philippines, Allan was returning to his hotel in Cebu with some mates when Editha and her friends strolled by, returning home from the beach. The girls stopped at a street stall to buy some snacks and one of Allan's mates stopped to chat to one of Editha's friends. Allan kept walking to the hotel and Editha made to move off down the street, calling to her friend to hurry up. Allan, his mind on a dip in the hotel pool, was likewise telling his mate to get a move on. But their friends stayed put, chatting away, and Editha and Allan walked back to the stall. Their attraction was instant and within a week they were tripping off together visiting different islands – and falling in love.

Eventually Allan had to return to Manila to renew his visa. He left Editha in Cebu and didn't know when or whether he was going to get back. But within a week, she had come up to Manila for a friend's wedding. Editha checked at the hotel at which Allan said he'd be staying, but was told he wasn't registered there. She was just about to leave when one of Allan's mates walked in and told her where Allan was. Manila's a very big, very busy place. Had Editha arrived at the hotel a moment later or left a moment earlier she might never have tracked him down.

Eighteen months later they were engaged to be married and Editha was about to move to Australia.

Editha's parents were worried at first. How was she going to cope with the different culture and being so far from her family and friends? 'But they let me go because they thought that maybe my future would be better in Australia than in the Philippines. My mum said, "Things will change for you. Maybe your life will be easier." She was happy but I was the only one in the household doing the tasks like getting water, washing and ironing. The younger children were at school and the older ones were off doing things because my parents could not afford to send us all to school. So my mother was a bit sad about that but happy at the same time. Her daughter was getting married, but someone was taking her away. And then her daughter would have a better life. It wasn't easy for them. They had mixed emotions.'

It was a hard decision for Editha to make. She thought about not going. 'I actually said to Allan, "Maybe I will follow you. I will stay here for a while." But I thought of the future and about having children and realised that in Australia my kids would have better opportunities.'

Editha and Allan then put in motion the slow-moving cogs of the immigration process, so much slower in the Philippines than in Australia. Both governments' bureaucracies seemed to require endless filling in of forms. 'We went through three months of gathering up paperwork, getting Allan's proof that he was not married, getting all my papers done,' recalled Editha. 'And then we were in Manila, at the pier, after returning by ship from Celon having obtained my paperwork and farewelled my family. He was looking after all the luggage and I put my overnight bag down briefly. There were lots of people and when I went to pick it up again, it had disappeared with all my papers in it. Maybe they thought I had money. I was with Allan so they thought I was loaded, I guess. We weren't. We had to start again with all the paperwork.'

It would have been easier if they hadn't been doing it all on the cheap, doing it all themselves, rather than employing an agent because they had no money. But they finally made it out of the Philippines and travelled to Sydney via Bangkok, which was the cheapest route they could find. This was Editha's first trip away from home and the week-long, honeymoon-style holiday in Bangkok is a time she remembers fondly.

Editha left off reminiscing when she realised the drive to Reuben's home town seemed to be taking longer than expected. Craig became concerned they might even be lost. 'The guide told us it would take an hour, and after three and a half hours I was thinking, let's just turn back,' said Craig. 'And then the road seemed to get smaller and smaller and smaller and we were going down little tracks and we just thought, nah, we're not going to get there. Let's turn around. But about fifteen minutes later we got to the place. And even then, it didn't actually front the street. You had to go up this little lane, up the side of someone else's house to get to their house. We were going up the little lane and I was thinking, this isn't it. We've come all this way for nothing.'

But they hadn't come for nothing. Indeed there was a big surprise waiting for them as they got out of the car. Reuben wasn't at sea, he was right there standing outside his home, peering in bewilderment through the darkness, as a group of people – one holding a camera – walked towards him.

'He was looking around and I sort of recognised him from when he'd visited Sydney,' Craig said. 'But I didn't want to say anything because he wasn't expecting us. I just stood back until he saw Mum. And he's going, "What's going on? Who are all these people? What do you want?" But straight away he's inviting us to come in, even though he didn't know who we were. His natural instinct was to say, "Come inside, come inside." I thought that was fantastic. And he's looking around still and all of a sudden he goes, "Oh my God! That's my sister!" And then he saw me.'

'I thought he would be overseas, on an oil tanker,' said Editha. 'We were sure he would be away. I was going to visit his wife and kids. But it was so fantastic to see him.'

Reuben was overwhelmed with emotion at seeing his sister. Every time he tried to express how happy he was to see her, he wept. So did Editha. All she could do was hug him.

It's not uncommon for busy families to find it difficult to keep in touch as much as they'd like, and for communication to come in infrequent letters and yearly birthday or Christmas phone calls. Editha had to try to keep track of eight brothers and sisters. Plus, of course, she had to keep up with her five children. She still worked early

Editha reunited with her brother Reuben and his wife, Pacing

shifts for Qantas at the airport and kept her house running like clockwork. She was undeniably a busy woman, but still, she felt remorseful now as she sat there with Reuben that she had not had more contact over the years.

'I didn't know all my nieces' and nephews' names because I just never get around to writing. For me, life goes on. I don't have time. And then when I do have time, I don't know what to write. I remembered one or two of my nieces and nephews. But that's all. That's why it was a shock for Craig. It was like, "Wow, look at all these cousins." He was surprised at how many of them there were.'

'I felt somewhat like an intruder and a little bit embarrassed because I didn't know them,' said Craig. 'But after talking to them and finding out more about them and how directly related I was to them, and getting to see what good people they are, I felt like I had gained something and I wanted to give something back. I never got to find out too much about them or say as much as I would have liked to them. But I'm sure I'll see them again. And I'll get my chance to give something back.

'We have a very big family and because there are so many people in our immediate family, when you do get time to yourself, you take it for yourself. We're always interacting with everyone else, Mum, Dad, my sisters, and them with me. Moments that you can have to yourself become so much more crucial. So our extended family ties have maybe suffered for that. But it's great to re-establish them.'

Craig had already given Reuben something, though, just by being there. His uncle, who just happened to be wearing a Sydney T-shirt when Craig and Editha arrived, was one of the few family members in the Philippines who was really aware of Craig's football career. 'His ship came over to Sydney a few years back and he went to watch a game,' said Editha. 'And he thought it was great.'

'Sitting in the Sydney football stadium, with a huge crowd, he was pretty blown away that I was one of the people running around on the field, and I think I scored a couple of tries,' laughed Craig. 'He'd never been to Sydney before. He saw where we lived and there were posters around with my photo on it. He couldn't get enough stuff to take back with him. They don't know what Rugby League is over there, but he sort of conveyed the general idea across to the rest of the family. There was a Roosters poster and a South Sydney poster at his house.'

'He showed us his kids' room and said, "Look, Craig, look at your photo",' said Editha. 'And they had a big poster of him which I had given him when he was in Sydney. It's still in good condition. It made me very happy.'

Craig and Editha returned briefly to the chaos of Manila before heading out to the beautiful heart of the Philippines and Cebu. Along the way they broke their journey at the island of Bohol, the home of the famous Chocolate Hills, an incredible range of almost identical, startlingly dark brown hills that derive their unusual colour from the lawn-like ferny growth that covers them. 'In summer the vegetation goes brown, dark brown, like chocolate,' smiled Editha, taking in the familiarity of the extraordinary landscape.

The trip was proving to be a whirlwind, but along the way Craig was getting a taste of the diversity and beauty of the country. As Bohol also boasted some of the best diving in the Philippines, Craig took time out to snorkel in the blue-topaz water rimmed by talc-white sand.

But Craig and Editha's minds were really on family matters now, and both were eager to resume their journey to Editha's hometown.

Cebu City is the second biggest city in the Philippines and the country's busiest port. For decades travellers have used Cebu as a base to explore the Vasayas, the Philippines' main island group. From Cebu it's only a short trip to the popular beaches of Moalboal and Bantayan, favourite haunts for backpackers and seekers of paradise. Since Editha visited her hometown eleven years ago the number of travellers, port traffic and the local population had all grown enormously. Cebu had always been a busy place, but now Editha feared home might have become foreign to her.

'I don't really remember what it looks like,' said

Editha. 'It has been a long time. But I can say that it is not really picturesque, not really a destination. Tourists go there to use it as a base and travel out to the provinces. I have heard everyone say Cebu is better now though: better shops and hotels, and the roads are better. I've heard that life is better for people there.'

Life might have been a little bit better for people in Cebu, but in the Philippines the gap between the haves and the have-nots remains vast. Unrestrained development and environmental destruction is also rife, the result of old colonial exploitation perpetuated by local corruption. Many of the Philippines' seven thousand islands have been all but denuded of forest, the subsequent soil erosion ruining agricultural areas. The island of Cebu is one of the most profoundly affected: ninety-nine per cent of its native vegetation is gone. Open sewers run by front doors. There are homeless and beggars everywhere. Makeshift shantytowns of cardboard and discarded scrap are home to the elderly, infants and all ages in between.

Editha's parents are among the have-nots on Cebu. When Editha lived there life had been far from easy. But it was what she had been used to, and when she was on the verge of leaving for Australia for the first time she had feared the loss of all that was familiar.

'I was worried,' said Editha, 'because I didn't know anybody in Australia. I was a bit doubtful. Was it going to be worse than the Philippines or better? I just had no idea.'

When she arrived in Australia, Editha found the move had been for the better, but it did not come without challenges or homesickness. 'There were many things that were much easier. When you wanted to cook, you didn't have to go outside and light up the firewood. To wash our clothes in Cebu, we had to get up early and walk miles to wash in the river. Those things were a lot different in Australia and so much easier. But still, it was hard for me because I didn't know anybody and even things like the food; I was not used to it. Baked beans, steak; that was not my type of food. There was nowhere, it seemed, that I could get Filipino food.' Then another Filipino lady moved in right across the road. 'She had been in Australia for a long time and she showed me where I could shop. I had been in Australia two years by then, but once I realised I could get Filipino stuff in this country, things started changing. Everything was better. I didn't miss the Philippines so much and realised that Australia was better than back home. Life in Australia was a lot better.'

The night before returning to Cebu, Editha's thoughts wound back to the days before she left and the life she might have led had she not married Allan and gone to Australia. She wondered about the lives her children might have led had she stayed in the Philippines. It was impossible to guess how things would have turned out for them. All she knew was that she was grateful her kids had grown up with the privileges of an Australian upbringing. Anyway, now was not the time to dwell on the past. She was getting ready to see her parents again.

'I couldn't sleep,' Editha said the next morning as they

set off for Cebu. 'I was tossing and turning. All I want to do: I just want to see them. That's all.'

'I'm excited for her,' said Craig, 'because I know that as soon as she meets her family they'll be as close as they ever were.'

Driving through Cebu City's maze of overcrowded streets and furious traffic, the contrasts between Craig's world of opportunity back in Sydney and the harsh reality of life on Cebu appeared before him in razor-sharp clarity. The images around him brought back memories of his childhood visit to the Philippines.

'I remember that it wasn't too flash,' Craig said of his impressions of Cebu as a six-year-old. 'It wasn't like the picturesque postcard islands that you see when you go to the travel agents. It was more like downtown Bangkok. My grandparents' place was on a main road and there was not a lot for a kid my age to do. I made a few friends and we knocked around and got into a lot of mischief. I remember open sewers and pigs and chickens and back alleys where we got into trouble. I remember sleeping on the floor under mosquito nets. And I remember it was very hot.

'I don't really remember my grandfather. I remember my grandmother as being a largish woman. I remember an uncle that would sit me on the front of an old bike and dink me down to the markets. He stacked it once and I nearly got run over but I never told Mum and Dad.

'But mostly, I guess, I remember the kids in the area around the same age as me that I hung around with.'

Craig was hoping he'd meet up with some of those kids who'd be grown men now, and was eager to return to his grandparents' home to see how his distant memories matched the reality. 'I do remember there was a tree in the backyard that had the most unbelievable fruit. I have never tasted it since. I'm looking forward to seeing if it's still there.'

For Editha, the contrast between memory and reality confronted her as soon as they entered her parents' neighbourhood. As they walked down the street on which she once lived, Editha searched for familiar sights and found so much had changed that she really did not recognise the place.

'Before I left, the houses all had big gardens,' said Editha. 'Now they are all squeezed in. They made the road wider and built an overpass. It looked so different to me. Craig had a better memory of it than I did. I was saying to Craig, "Where is my home?" Luckily, he has a good memory. He said, "Mum, I think we passed your place. It's back there." I was looking for certain landmarks but you couldn't see them any more because there'd been so much development. All these places had been built in front of the things I was looking for. There were all these shops and factories blocking out the old sights. It looked completely different.'

The greatest shock for Editha came when they reached her family's home. Recognition turned to dismay when she saw how dreadfully rundown it was. 'Oh my God,' Editha said over and over as she walked along the laneway down the side of her childhood home. 'Oh my God.'

Editha stood at what used to be the front gate and called out, 'Ma . . . Ma . . .' There was no response. Because their visit was to be a surprise, there was no one listening out for them, no one running out to welcome them. Some children on their way to school came walking down the laneway and she asked them where the entrance to the property was. It was distressing to have to do that, like some kind of stranger.

But when Editha called at the new entrance and saw her mother emerge from the house, all distress melted

After 11 years apart, Editha's parents are overwhelmed with joy at seeing their daughter and grandson again

away in the excitement of reunion. The sounds of happy surprise filled the air and Editha was delighted to discover not just her mum and dad home, but cousins and nephews. Back in her mother's arms after eleven years, Editha wept for joy.

Craig, this big strapping man from Sydney, towered over all of them. But he was humbled in the presence of his grandfather and grandmother as he witnessed their love for their daughter, his mother. Still in a state of shock, Craig's grandfather overcame his tears and shyness and embraced Craig, hugging his grandson with all the force of sixteen years' worth of love.

Later that day Craig's cousin, Frederick, one of the kids with whom he'd got into so much trouble all those years ago, showed him around the neighbourhood. As they walked down the streets surrounding his grandparents' home, Craig was followed by gaggles of school children and waved at by admiring women. Some even asked to have their pictures taken with him. 'I think that was more about the cameras than me,' said Craig. 'And all the white people.'

Here he wasn't a football hero, he was a celebrity just because he was different. He was a curiosity.

Craig's curiosity had been on overdrive all day, too. 'Everything was so much smaller than I remembered it,' laughed Craig. 'Sitting in my grandparents' lounge room back when I was six, I thought it was huge. When I got

In Cebu Craig wasn't a celebrity because he was a football hero – he was a curiosity

there, having grown up, I felt like I was in a cubby house.'

There was a well outside the house that Allan had installed for the family sixteen years ago. Craig remembered looking up to it. Now, of course, it didn't even reach his waist. But the new perspective brought more than spatial disorientation; it brought a clear view to Craig of just how fortunate he was to have lived the kind of life he had so far. His landscape had been the beach, big backyards and massive grassy public spaces where kids could play and run and kick a ball around forever. In Cebu City, such luxuries did not exist.

A new overpass had been built to accommodate the

Young Craig beside the well

city's increasing population and traffic. The overpass cut halfway through the front yard of Editha's childhood home. 'My dad did not want to lose his land but the government had made its decision and it didn't matter if you owned the land, if the government said to you, "This is what we want and this is how much you'll get for it," if you didn't accept, you got nothing.'

Years ago Allan had put a lot of work into improving Editha's parents' property by doing the place up and landscaping the vacant lot next to theirs to create a beer garden, so that Editha's parents could make a living instead of having to rely on their children's financial support. Now the garden was gone, the building was in a state of disrepair and there were people squatting on Editha's family's land beneath the overpass.

Editha's family were quiet, modest people, who never liked to rock the boat, and their world and livelihood had been ravaged by aggressive officials. Allan's attitude to this injustice was succinct: 'They were just taken to the cleaners. It was as simple as that.'

For Editha, who was seeing all this devastation first-hand, the injustice was hard to take. 'I feel very sad,' she said. 'I am happy to see my mum and dad, but I didn't want to see this. I didn't want to see this place in this state. I thought I was going to be more happy, and not sad. It didn't really turn out the way I wanted.'

And Craig noted that the tree he remembered in the backyard no longer bore any fruit.

But here Editha and Craig had harvested a new crop of memories, some sad, others joyful. The confrontation Craig had nervously anticipated had turned out to be very real, but with it would come blessings for them both . . .

At the end of their trip, Editha's extended family gathered for a picnic at one of Cebu's better beaches. There Craig learned he had many more relatives than he'd thought he had – enough to field a few football teams it seemed. As they all lined up for a family photo Craig felt part of something greater than himself, a feeling beyond the connections he shared within his immediate family back in Sydney. He was part of a world network of people who shared his heritage.

The whole family gathers for a picnic at the beach

'The older you get, the more appreciative you are that you've got something in another part of the world,' he said.

Walking through his grandparents' neighbourhood afterwards, he found himself surrounded by Filipino kids once more, all mugging happily for the camera. Craig reflected on how different his life would have been had he been one of them. But then again, he thought maybe it wouldn't have been all bad to have grown up in Cebu. 'I remember when I was a kid I didn't know any different and I just liked running around here with all the other kids. I suppose if you don't know any different, it's just fine. I had always been a bit nervous at the prospect of coming back here, and maybe a bit embarrassed at this side of things with my family. But now, I feel that it just adds another dimension to me. The more you learn, the more you realise these things are just another part of you and that's a positive thing.'

Above all, Craig was grateful to have had the opportunity to see his grandmother and grandfather. He hoped it wouldn't be the last time he saw them, but both were nearing eighty and he was aware how timely this visit might have been. Through tears of happiness his grandfather said in his broken English, 'I am very happy they

Editha and Craig with Editha's parents, Cornelio and Amada

came back. My life is complete now. If I die, then they cannot see me. They cannot come back. So I give thanks, a million thanks, for having them here in the Philippines.'

This was the heart of the journey for Editha. 'My dad had had a stroke,' she said. 'He looked good, better than I expected. But the reality was, it might have been the last time I saw him. He is so very thankful to have seen us. And I am more thankful than I can say to have seen him. Even with the heartbreak of seeing the property like it was, it was worth it just to see my mum and dad.'

Back home in Sydney, Craig's crazy schedule immediately kicked in, as did Editha's. The likelihood of them spending time alone like that again was slim. But in their hearts they would cherish their Philippines experience forever.

'Some of my best memories were obviously meeting the family,' said Craig, 'seeing how everyone had changed, and trying to remember who was who and what contact I had with them when I was over there the last time.

'But also spending time with my mum. I get very little chance to spend time with her. When we're in Sydney, it's always with the rest of the family. I never have my mum to myself. So I really enjoyed going to the falls and different places and just hanging out. It was probably the thing that I liked about it the most and will remember most clearly.'

For a few months life went on as busy as ever for the

Wing family, but Editha's joy at having seen her parents again and Craig's deep appreciation of the experience, prompted Allan to take Editha back to Cebu, this time with their daughters Danielle, Taryn and Kirsty. Annabelle had already made a trip of her own. 'I saw Editha's father on the video and when he said his life was complete because he'd seen Craig, I felt it was a bit unfair that there were two of the kids he had never seen,' said Allan. 'And Danielle was only about two years of age when he last saw her. So I thought, I've got to do the right thing and take the other kids back to him, and at the same time let them see him before he passes away.'

'My father was so happy,' said Editha after the second trip, her eyes sparkling at the memory of him surrounded by his granddaughters. For Editha, seeing her parents again remained the absolute highlight of both trips. 'Seeing my mum and dad, seeing that they were still alive, I was really happy. That was the most important thing.'

Craig wasn't able to join his family on that trip; his training schedule didn't allow it. But he didn't discount visiting again some day. 'I just really appreciate knowing that they're there now. It's added something to my life in a very subtle way. I mean, I always knew they were there, but having a material connection is a really great thing.'

Those subtleties have enriched him and the experience has reaffirmed something else he already knew: 'You see a lot of things over there and it makes you realise how lucky you are.'

The images and emotions that had been captured on film would continue to remind Craig of this experience.

'It really wasn't till I saw the documentary back home that it all sank in,' he said. 'My grandmother hadn't changed much at all. She'd aged very well. My grandfather, I could see that he had aged. It felt really important to spend time with them as an adult, let them see me as an adult and know basically that, though I live all those kilometres away, they are part of me. And for me, it's just nice to know that they're there and that I've seen them.

'It's an experience, and these kinds of experiences will always make your life better,' he said. 'No matter how you react to it, it's something that you've done. Our family's travelled all over Asia, we've seen the poorer side of things, so I wasn't totally shocked when I went there. I was just shocked at how different it was to how I remembered it. How much more populated it was than before. When I was there last, it was probably as densely populated as my parents' street in Maroubra. Now, it's like a place in the middle of Parramatta Road. I remember when I was there as a kid, I used to go to all the vacant lots with my cousins and there were lots of different places you could go. But now there's shops and houses and whatever. Seeing that kind of change just opens your eyes, shows you how the world changes, and lets you know about your own good fortune.'

Allan is pleased and proud at the ways the trip nourished his son. 'He got to see the other side and how his relatives live and I think that has given him even more appreciation of what he has here. I think it has made him try that much harder in making the most of it. When he saw how tough they were doing it over there and the lack of opportunity, it just reminded him of how lucky he is. We've always brought up our kids to be appreciative of their lives. And Craig's always kept that appreciation. But it's good to be reminded like that. So long as he doesn't become complacent, he's going to keep going a long way, especially with the knowledge of where he's come from and who he is. He's aware that it's all just making up the greater whole of who he is. You can't have the positives without the negatives. Family life is like that. Anything is like that. And the experience of going over there, seeing his family, that's helped him prepare for life.'

Allan is also chuffed for Editha, the shy, humble woman who never took much glory from her own achievements as a mum or otherwise. 'She felt a lot of pride in being able to show off her son to her relatives back there, though she'd never say it,' laughed Allan. 'She got to show them not only Craig, but what's become of her and what she's been able to produce in her life by coming out here to Australia. She *is proud* of those achievements. And it was good for her to publicly acknowledge that.'

The documentary has well and truly blown Editha's cover – now everyone knows she is Craig Wing's mum. 'After the documentary was screened, at work they said to me, "We didn't know your son is Craig Wing",' said Editha, laughing. But her modesty about her famous son remains as unwavering as ever. 'I don't like to say anything because I don't know what people will think of me, saying who he is like that.'

This is no false modesty. It is a gift of character that she has inherited from her parents. Editha Wing's focus has always been on the strength of her children's characters, not how much applause they might receive. 'Craig is a good kid,' she said. 'What he has he deserves because he has worked hard for it. He's just a good kid and I hope he stays that way. Some kids, when they do well, their attitude changes, but I am hoping Craig stays the way he is, just natural and good to everyone.'

It might be hard for him not to with the threat of Allan's size eight and a half boot on the backside.

The one thing you can rely on . . . is change.

GEORGE CUMINE

Wendy Matthews
Canadian Australian

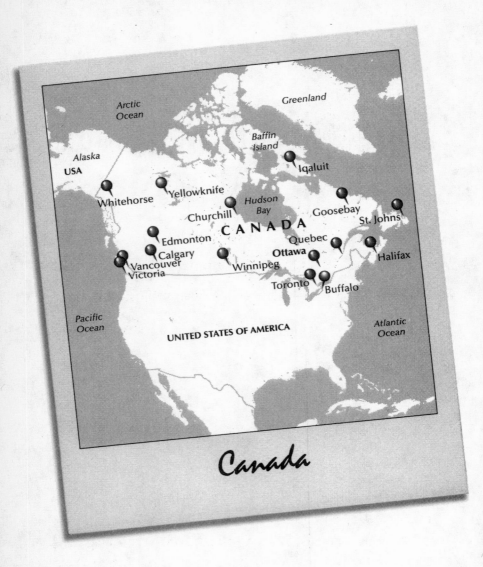

Canada

Filling the
Empty Cup

'I get so much out of going back. And sometimes in my life, you know, all I want to do is go and curl up in my mother's wedding dress or something . . . But I realised that Australia is my home. It is that simple . . . And that complex.'

When Wendy Matthews was fifteen, she packed a bag and told her mum she was going busking for a few weeks.

Wendy's mother Joan Matthews can vividly recall that day, over twenty years ago. 'I felt awful. I just felt sad and very, very concerned for her because she was not yet sixteen. We sat up all the night before, talking and crying. But she just said, "I have to go." And then I saw her off. I remember her hair was very long and she had on a very long skirt. And I knew she was going out of my life somehow. She said she was only going away for a very short period of time. But it turned out to be what I thought it was going to be, which was almost forever.

'I felt a great, great, great loss. My three children were always very independent and had things they had to do in life. As a parent you had to accept that and, luckily, I realised that this was what love was: giving the person just what they needed.

'But that didn't mean it didn't hurt. It hurt terribly.'

Of course, back then, Wendy had no idea just how things would turn out. 'I didn't plan it that way,' said Wendy. 'My mother and I are particularly close, so I think we both would have had a very hard time had I really consciously made that decision of: all right, I'm leaving home now to see what the world holds and I'm going away forever.'

But, as an adult, in the cosy Bondi flat she'd called home for fifteen years, so far away from her family in Canada, she found herself reflecting more and more. She realised now, it wasn't just youthful willfulness that made her leave home, though that played a large part in it. She hadn't seen it as a teen, but as an adult she clearly saw that there were deeper reasons behind her decision to leave. And she hadn't been the only one to leave: her two brothers, Glenn and Gary, had flown the nest not long after she did.

'My father and mother split up when I was about fourteen, and we really kind of exploded all over the world,' said Wendy. 'We've never come together to live as a whole again.'

Also coming into play at that time was the incredible

force of Wendy's teenage identity, striving like mad to find its place in the world. 'Ever since I was this big, people have said "You look just like your mother." I was convinced that we were somehow the same person. And then it was like, well, hold on, if I'm not her, which I'm not, then who am I? That was also a catalyst for me leaving when I did. In a very unconscious way it was something that had to happen.'

Wendy headed southwest with friends a year after her parents' separation, hitting Mexico for a while, where days turned into weeks and then into months. Next she travelled to southern California, and thanks to her distinct, velvety voice, soon she was able to give up the busking and began to pick up good quality gigs, working with some of the world's top vocalists. And the months turned into years: seven years in Los Angeles in fact.

In 1983, still based in LA, she was singing backup vocals for Glenn Shorrock, an Australian who had enjoyed huge success in the US as the lead vocalist in the Little River Band. Glenn suggested she tour to his home-land with him. To Wendy it seemed like a great gig. 'I had been in travel mode. I just kind of went where travel and opportunities took me,' she said. But she was in for so much more than just a nice working holiday down under. She didn't know it then, but she was coming home. And the years would turn into decades.

'When I got here I realised I was much healthier and happier out of Los Angeles,' said Wendy. 'When you live there you tend to forget there's anything beyond the walls of LA. Every cab driver's really an actor or a singer and everybody is constantly on this treadmill that you don't really think about till you get out. Australia was much, much more to my pace and my sensibilities. It was so different. Coming also from the land of huge shopping malls, I loved little fruit and veg shops and butchers. It sounds so simple but I found it such a lovely place.

'And I'd been in a seven-year relationship and it wasn't going too well. I saw an opportunity to start again and live a bit more of my own life. I don't know why, but it just wasn't an option to go back home to Montreal. And I didn't know quite what I was going to do but I felt like I had to keep going somehow.'

Wendy's decision to stay in Australia might have been born of an inexplicable compulsion to follow an undefined destiny, but it proved to be a fortuitous one. She established herself on the Australian music scene as a unique talent and Australians loved her soulful, sensuous voice, her ethereal elegance and the way she sang with heartfelt emotion. She had artistic honesty and a down-to-earth charisma; an everyman connection that attracted fans from all walks of life.

In no other country, not the United States, not even the country of her birth, Canada, had Wendy Matthews enjoyed the kind of success that was hers in Australia. With seven ARIAs (Australian Recording Industry Association Awards), multiple hit singles and albums, and sell-out tours, she was the most popular female performer in Australia throughout much of the nineties.

Fate gave her little choice but to stay in Australia.

Despite the tyranny of distance, Wendy's family was

as loving and caring as the next, perhaps even more so *because* of that distance. Indeed, it was because they had all been so close in the first place that the sudden eruption in the family created a new dynamic that they all felt acutely and to which they responded accordingly. It didn't mean they loved each other any less. It was more that some chain reaction had been set in motion by the breakup of Wendy's parents, Joan and Peter, and it put them all on different trajectories. They had been a household full of strong individuals and, in retrospect, it seemed as if separation was always going to happen, whatever the catalyst.

Wendy did, however, find herself comparing, sometimes enviously, the more compact lives of other families to her scattered one. 'Things like Christmas and Mother's Day are just so hyped up and you're so reminded that you're far away from home and you're alone and it's all about family and you don't have any and rah-rah-rah,' she said with a laugh. 'But all my friends in Australia, you know, they're rolling their eyes, "I gotta go to my parents' place for lunch." I don't know if it's taking things for granted, but the whole family thing often seems such a burden for people who live close by.'

Not for Wendy, who every day had to deal with the reality of not being able to pop home to Mum's for a cup of tea and a chat.

'Sometimes it just seems absurd that we're scattered all over the place. There's a feeling with the passing of time, especially with my parents, that there is not all that much time; there is not forty to sixty years. And it does seem absurd that we are so far apart and we are not together while we can be.'

Over the past fifteen years Wendy had travelled to Canada as often as she could, even if her stays had to be short, because as much as life had led her elsewhere, she was far from disconnected from the home of her birth. She felt deeply gratified by having made Australia her new home, a place where her art had been allowed to flourish. But she also craved the warmth of her family in Canada, and when she went home that's exactly what she got.

'I find Canada very nurturing somehow,' she said. 'It's all about my family and my mother. When I go back, I am usually at the end of my tether and it always fills up the empty cup.'

Though her mother had been out to Australia, it had been three years since Wendy had been back to Canada when she decided to join Eden and Nicola Gaha, cameraman Dave Kelly and his photographer wife Joanna to make a documentary of her journey home for *The Ties That Bind*. But as excited as she was about seeing her two brothers, their partners and her nephews, and especially her mother Joan, she also found herself fretting a little about this trip. There was a lot on her mind as she prepared for the journey.

They had decided it would be great to surprise her

family members; to turn up at their houses without warning and to do so with cameras rolling. Having enjoyed fame in Australia, Wendy had long been careful to respect the privacy and feelings of her family. She had never exploited personal relationships for publicity. This documentary, of course, was a different matter. She had agreed to be involved in it because the television series was not gratuitous exposure of matters personal. It had a point and purpose. It explored notions that had, pretty much all her adult life, been her motivations: notions of home, identity, family, belonging. She had already heard about the journeys of others in the series, and Wendy felt she would have much to gain from taking a similar pilgrimage herself.

'It seemed a wonderful exercise, such a special opportunity; to have time set aside for this journey with the specific purpose of exploring emotions about certain aspects of my life,' she said. 'What kept popping into my mind were situations like Princess Diana dying and the way the whole world was crying over it. It seemed to me that those situations came to be about more than just the person who had died. It became universal permission to grieve; a safe time and place for everybody to feel and acknowledge emotions that they might not have stopped to feel otherwise. And in a sense, that was what the whole trip was about for me. Permission to feel the emotion.'

For Wendy, journeys homeward had always intensified long-held feelings of alienation. Living in Australia had meant she always felt a slight sense of otherness.

And yet when she visited her family on the other side of the world, she felt like an Australian in Canada. This was nothing new to her. Even as a child that sense of otherness was with her. She had been more comfortable in her imaginings and her heritage than in her home. 'I was a dreaming child,' she said. And the Native American blood that ran amid her Scottish, Spanish and Cajun background was the stuff of her dreams. Sometimes, it felt more real than her suburban Montreal life had done.

'I don't mean to sound negative here, but a part of me had never felt at home in Canada,' she said. 'For instance, my father had never really known what to make of me, ever since I was tiny. So I never felt quite at home at home. And in Australia, as much as I love it, I've definitely always felt a little bit like an alien.'

Then when her parents separated, home felt stranger to her still. Despite her young sense of being different (and she was different, a star in the making), Wendy had loved her childhood: both parents present and accounted for, her grandfather George living not far away, wrestling with her brothers by the lake, hearing the calls of the wolves and watching the cycle of four strong seasons, exploring the places where the Native Canadians hunted and fished. 'The feeling of it is still something I aspire to,' said Wendy. 'If I really want to be in my full potential, I think of those formative years and I always try to get back there, to some sort of essence of that, always.'

There had been a distinct final chapter to those formative years and that idyllic childhood, a prelude to her parents' separation. Peter, her father, had organised a family road trip in a last effort to capture a sense of togetherness. Wendy was thirteen, her brother Glenn twelve and brother Gary fourteen, and they weren't too happy about the idea. 'School was just out and at that age we were just wanting to hit the summer streets and hang out with our pals and just say "See you later." But my father came home and he'd sold our car and bought a van with all the camping gear in it,' and she paused to laugh and adopt a hillbilly twang '. . . and we were driving to California.'

'And we kicked and screamed, but it was one of the most extraordinary memories that I've got of our family all being together, driving along across Canada and across the States, through Arizona and the Grand Canyon. All those adventures. It was an extraordinary thing he did.'

Something had happened in her family, though. A fissure that would play out its natural course, despite the last ditch effort to keep it all together by a man and his van, a year before he left the family home for good.

'It was sort of our last dance, though none of us knew it at the time. And though I wasn't fully aware of it in an intellectual sense because I was thirteen, I was hyper-sensitive to people's unconscious stuff, a lot more than I was comfortable with,' said Wendy. 'And it became very clear later, from an adult perspective, that during that whole trip, as much as I loved it, my shoulders were up around my ears, because I felt so strongly what was going on with my mother.

'And my father. I remember opening up one eye,

driving late, late at night and looking at my father and almost wanting to cry, thinking, all he wants is to be at the helm, in the driver's seat with his family around him and right now he's just loving life. He's revelling in it right now, because he's got his wife silent by his side and his kids contained and cosy and he's at the helm. He was having a quiet moment with himself, and for me it was just a flash of a recognition there. And it struck me as rather sad, too, because he was trying to hold it together and I don't even think he realised it then.

'What I tend to remember from that trip were anecdotes: rattlesnakes and bears jumping out of trees; I guess what a thirteen-year-old would remember. But as an adult now, I'm so aware of all the other stuff that was going on. Those anecdotal memories were crystal clear, I realised, because I was hanging on. I was trying to take in everything because somehow I knew that this was it. And it was true. Shortly after that we all just exploded around the world and we never came back.'

All of Wendy's family now lived in Canada except for her. But Canada was a big country and they were pretty much spread out across it – only Gary and Joan lived near to each other. She wondered, with all of them splitting up like that, how they would feel about putting their family relationships in the way of the camera's lens. Would they feel, as she did, that such examination was a positive thing?

'On the plane there, during all the sort of anticipating, pre-meeting-up stuff, the whole time I was thinking, how are they going to feel? And how are they going to deal with this? I hope they're okay and not uncomfortable,' said Wendy.

'I can't say I was used to it; it had taken me a long time to not be so aware of cameras and things, to just relax. I realised you had to completely get out of your own way; which was the case in being able to relax about most things, I suppose. I knew that, but I was just consumed with thinking, how will my family deal with this? How will they feel about this?

'But of course, you learned the most in life through dealing with relationships. Just by thinking about them, my relationships with them, how I cared about them, I realised that you just had to trust that everybody was going to handle it the way they were going to handle it. You couldn't pull your hair out worrying about all that stuff. You just had to let go trying to control it. And you either did what you intended or you didn't.

'And I had to go through with the trip, because being afforded the opportunity, having a catalyst specifically to look into the past and family, that was really very special. And to have an actual excuse for everybody to do it, it seemed it could be done so much more freely because there were guidelines. Someone had said, "Okay, you're allowed to do this." I just had to take that opportunity.'

She did, however, at the last minute draw the line at surprising her mother. Wendy decided it would be best to warn her. Though Joan was an almost seventy, yoga-teaching, spiritually evolved force of nature, she was still Wendy's mother. And one who would want to be prepared for guests – especially guests with a video camera. Wendy didn't feel she could put her on the spot like that.

The boys, Glenn and Gary, well, when all was said and done, when the angst and anticipation were put aside, there was still the fact that they were her brothers, after all. The Matthews kids had never really grown out of the urge to tease each other. They might just be fun to surprise.

When Wendy went home to Canada, she usually went by way of Los Angeles. She always took the opportunity to visit old friends from her days living there. From LA she would fly to Montreal in Canada's east, the city in which she grew up. And from Montreal she would drive an hour to the small town of Sutton where her grandfather had lived, where her family had a weekender on a lake and where her mother and older brother Gary now lived. But Wendy's first stop on this trip with Eden and the crew was to be a surprise call-in on her younger brother Glenn who lived and worked in the Alberta Rockies, right across the other side of the enormous Canadian chunk of the North American continent. So they were flying into Vancouver in Canada's southwest corner, from where they would catch a connecting flight to Calgary before completing a road trip to Glenn's small town of Canmore.

They had a two-hour wait ahead of them in Vancouver before boarding the next flight. Wendy seldom went to Vancouver and there was someone in this city she rarely saw. She called him up and he came to the airport to meet her. It was her dad Peter.

'I really never felt like he understood me, but I adored him,' said Wendy. 'I thought he was an amazing human being and he'd always been an artist which I very much appreciated having grown up with. I loved his sort of Hunter S. Thompson-esque thing,' she said of her photographer father's adventurous, unconventional streak.

It had been five years since she had seen her dad, and that last time was in Australia. And yet, she recognised the silhouette of him, dark against the background of the grand, floor-to-ceiling glass wall of the airport terminal. He was different, of course, and the vision of him that came into focus as she ran towards him to give him a hug made Wendy acutely aware of the passage of time and the tyranny of distance.

'Not seeing people all the time as I did, you saw your parents ageing from one meeting to the next. And when you saw them, at first it was a real shock. But within five minutes you knew that you were you and they were they, and I knew that they did the same to me.'

Of course they recognised each other's essence, because some things never changed. There he was, dressed just like a Canadian, she smiled to herself: outdoorsy. Sensible shoes, walking shorts, a light, sturdy, sensible jacket. Clothes just right for clambering around taking pictures. He was still a photographer. Still her dad. His energy was still strong and his physicality robust. She hugged him and laughed happily.

But not so far beneath the happiness there was that same thing as always, just holding it back from being complete joy. After so many years, they were still the same people dealing with the same old stuff they always had. The meeting was a short one, over coffee in an airport Starbucks. And yet, like every time Wendy saw her dad, that 'stuff' took no time to arise, sending her emotions back to her childhood home, to Montreal, to the time when she was fourteen and her father left home. She didn't talk about it on the trip, but a year later, reflecting on the experience, she found the emotional space to articulate that undercurrent.

'Although my father was the one to leave, the separation was essentially instigated by my mother's withdrawal from their relationship,' Wendy said of the breakdown of her parents' marriage. She spoke carefully, delicately, more and more quietly, as if speaking too loud or forcefully about the time might aggravate the old hurts. They were tender enough as they were. 'My mother was a completely different person then. She would have handled it a lot differently now. But she just generally, quietly withdrew. And he had a really hard time of it. He had to leave. He came in one night to say goodnight. He said, "I'm going to stay with a friend for a few days," and that was it.

'I had a very difficult time with it. I took a lot of anger out on my father. Now I am horrified to think about some of the ways I took that anger out on him. My God, he was just going through his own stuff at the time. And children can be cruel. Under the guise of honesty, children can be cruel.'

But children, of course, were just going through their own stuff, too. And Wendy still found herself going through that stuff. The light, the air in Canada, her dad . . . it brought her back there, to being fourteen-year-old Wendy, missing her dad.

'I really love him a lot. I don't have any anger towards my father. I used to right up until a few years ago,' said Wendy. 'Now I've just got compassion for him and yet . . .' she trailed off. So many years on, she still found it difficult to express the thoughts, particularly to her father, because it was unfinished business.

One of the most painful aspects for Wendy was that she had also carried a sense of responsibility for the breakdown of her parents' marriage. A short while after Peter left the family home, Wendy went from Montreal to Toronto to stay with family friends for a holiday. It was there that fourteen-year-old Wendy overheard a telephone conversation, the topic of which was her parents' breakup. The reason given for the breakup in that conversation was Wendy's mother's feelings for another man.

'And I was like, "What?" I had a huge moment of, "Oh my God! I've been angry at the wrong person. I've just got to call him".'

Wendy did call her dad. 'I understand now why you've been having such a hard time,' she'd said. 'I understand why you left.' She recounted to her father what she had overheard.

'What are you talking about?' her father had responded. It was the first he had heard of it.

'So I was the one who told my father,' said Wendy. 'Nothing was said ever again. Nobody said, "It's okay. You didn't do this." And so there's still this element in my fourteen-year-old brain that says I split my parents up; I severed it for good. And because it's unresolved, I think that's part of the distance between my father and me. We can never quite talk about it. My mother and I are great about it. We've talked about this stuff and resolved it.

'But here, at my age, with my dad I can still be this fourteen-year-old. I can so easily be sent back to this one moment between my father and me.'

Wendy and her dad didn't talk about any of that, there at Vancouver airport. Though Eden, Nicola, Dave and Joanna had left them alone, this was not the time nor the place.

'But seeing him again was wonderful. I could look at him and see the man I adored and understand that parents were just people trying to do the best they could. Everybody mucked up.'

As she flew out, she looked down on Vancouver, the city to which he'd moved after the divorce and in which he had forged a new life and a new family, the scenery for act two of her dad's life. As a fellow grownup she felt nothing but love for her dad. And yet she felt a pang of regret as she winged her way to Calgary, for it was clear that her father felt he needed more connection with her.

'As I get older my attitudes to those issues that we

hold onto about different people that we love has changed; softened. My priorities have changed. Maybe I am projecting, but that's what I felt I saw in him.'

Maybe one day they'd resolve that unfinished business, she thought, in the right place, at the right time.

Wendy felt she was definitely back in Canada now, as she unpacked a few things for a hotel sleepover in Calgary before surprising her brother Glen in Canmore the following day.

'Crossing time zones, I can feel this tangible thing of changing hemispheres, and all of a sudden I'm acutely aware of accents. And just the Canadian way, it's so different from the Australian way. It's not an overt thing. But the air and light changes and I just feel this shift and click inside and it's, "Okay, we've got to be open to this way now." And I have a pretty good recollection of that way, but I realise that where I live, in Australia, that way is much more natural to me now.'

If any city in Canada showed the passage of time and how long she had been away, it was Calgary. Not so long ago the city was dominated by cowboy boots and Stetson hats. It had been a major cattle centre, flat grazing plains stretching out to its south, the Rockies not far to the west. But the discovery of oil in the Canadian province of Alberta had turned the city into an urban, high-tech energy industry centre full of high rises and smart restaurants.

Though less familiar than it had ever been to her, and far away from Montreal where she grew up, Calgary nonetheless reminded Wendy of what going home meant. It was not about rehashing old hurts. Or reassessing why she lived elsewhere. Her life had been forged in Australia. Whatever the initial, mostly unconscious motivations for leaving had been, it was away from Canada that destiny had taken her. It was away from Canada that her potential had blossomed. Had she stayed, would she have enjoyed the same success in Canada as she had in Australia? It was a moot point now. She lived in Australia. Her family had long accepted and supported her in that. That didn't mean they didn't miss her. And it didn't mean she didn't miss them, either. It was just the way it was.

With that grounding settled long ago, the experience of coming home to Canada had been almost exclusively and simply about getting her fill of those people she loved more than anyone in the world. Filling the empty cup with family.

And now, getting to Calgary, closer than three hours away from her brother, Wendy was overwhelmed with the anticipation of the sheer pleasure she would feel upon seeing him. Sleeping in a city hotel overnight was almost more than she could handle. In fact, she didn't do much sleeping; she just lay awake thinking of what was ahead.

'My younger brother and I, when we were very young, I'm sure we could communicate without talking. He's an exceptional human being and I haven't seen him for a long time. He came out to Australia in about '98 and we found my land together, and that was a particularly good omen for me when I bought it,' said Wendy of her property in Coffs Harbour. 'I can't wait to see him. It was all I could do to stop myself from calling him last night from the hotel.'

But in the car on the way to Canmore she was also nervous. 'It's a sense of is he going to be there? And is he going to be comfortable? And am I going to be comfortable? And what's that going to be like? But any way I can clap my eyes on him and get my arms around him is going to be great.'

Wendy adored both her brothers, and of Glenn, the youngest of this 'tight-knit little trio', she said, 'I've always thought of Glenn as someone who was just on this earth to play and remind people that everything is fun. That's what I get from him.'

It was with all these emotions that Wendy finally climbed the stairs to her brother's apartment, followed by Eden, Nicola, Joanna and Dave. And the camera. She stood for a moment at the door, bracing herself, listening for noise beyond the door. So, he was home. Then she knocked. A loud, deliberate, here-we-go knock.

'Aaaaaaahhh!!' Glenn answered the door, and yes, Glenn was surprised. 'Wendy! What the hey?' he said, looking somewhat bamboozled at her presence, and at the camera, as his sister bear-hugged him, saying, 'Surprise! Surprise!' over and over.

'Who's the, ah, entourage?' said Glenn, laughing. 'What, you just happened to be in the . . . continent!' He held her at arm's length. 'It's really you, right?'

All Wendy could say was 'Surprise!' and laugh with sheer joy.

And then Glenn's surprise gave way to the wonderful warmth of being with his sister. 'Oh my God. It's so good to see you,' he said and squeezed her, closing his eyes, forgetting the camera, just being in the moment of reuniting with his sister.

'So,' he finally said to the crew, 'I'm just making some lasagne. Wanna stay for dinner?'

Later that afternoon, Wendy stood drinking beers with her brother on his balcony with its panoramic view of the snow-capped national parks that surrounded Canmore. The stance of each sibling, the similar way they bent one knee and rested one hand on the balcony rail, spoke volumes of their ease with each other. They looked like pieces of a set; similar but not the same. They shared a litheness, strength of bone structure in their faces, sparkling, mischievous eyes that they got from their mother. And they shared history. No need to talk about any of that. It was just there, bonding them together. Wendy became childlike with her little brother, in that great way adults do sometimes: unselfconscious, easy to laugh, playful and loving.

'We're still kind of like kids when we get together, my brothers and I,' said Wendy. 'There's a real feeling of levity when we get together and yet there's this incredible thing to our relationships. It's so rich and sometimes deep and there's no word for it. Part of it is like you've only walked down the block for five minutes. It's an automatic pick up where you left off in a way. But

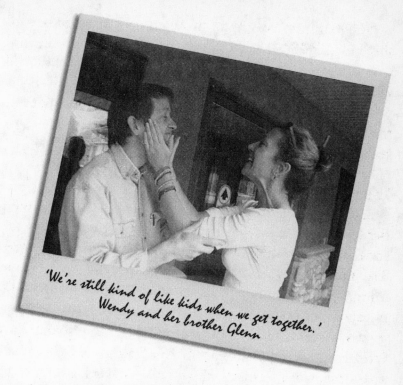

'We're still kind of like kids when we get together.'
Wendy and her brother Glenn

another part of it is this deep longing. I love seeing my
brothers. I just adore the boys. But it's really hard when
you don't see someone that often, because I see an older
person that's not quite the picture that I've got in my
head. I've got a very different picture from way back
when we were kids and teenagers, and that's how I think
of them, and when you're faced with this man again, it
magnifies the passage of time.'

But for two days they were kids once more. Wendy's
visit coincided with Glenn's birthday, and at a party to
mark the occasion, she saw him thrilled to receive from
a Canmore friend and fellow mountain climber a simple

yet poignant gift of a hand-drawn map showing the trail to a new secret ascent. It gladdened her heart to see him with friends who loved him like that. Knowing he lived with love made it easier being away. And she loved his passion for his landscape, which he shared with her throughout her stay, hiking and horse riding in the surreal beauty of the Alberta Rockies and having snow-ball fights in the spring cover.

But as she sat at the edge of one of the many astonishing, emerald-green lakes outside Banff, she explained to Eden, 'It's been beautiful to spend time here with Glenn. It's been great to see him and always, no matter how much time goes by, we just always fall into this easy thing. All day today I've been thinking, though, it's funny; how come I can't really enjoy today because I know we're leaving tomorrow? And I can't help but think, oh, I wonder when I'm going to see him next.'

Leaving was hard, as always. Well, harder than ever. 'I feel like I'm always saying goodbye either in Canada or back in Australia,' said Wendy. 'I know that's part of life. But it does get more difficult as you get older.'

Wendy and Glenn hugged and kissed and said goodbye, and with rueful smiles they let go of each other. Wendy had to take several deep breaths to keep the sobs at bay. Once in the car, there was nothing she could do to stop the tears; she put on her sunglasses and let them fall.

It was one a.m. when Wendy arrived in Montreal with Eden and company, and there was nothing for it but to go get pizza. As they walked through darkened streets of Canada's most romantic, European-style city, Wendy was brought back to the time when, barely in her teens, she sang Joni Mitchell and jazz standards in Montreal's bars. She'd had no choice *but* to sing – even back then, Joan and Peter had realised that – and here was where it all began.

The next day they were on their way to Sutton to see her mother. Wendy made a quick stop at her favourite wood-fired bagel shop, where she loaded up on a bag of one of Montreal's famed culinary delights. It was something she always did passing through. Indeed, for Wendy, going home meant happy indulgence in old patterns and memories. Doing the stuff she always did.

'There's this huge field out the back of my mother's house where I've been walking ever since I was one, and which I can't wait to get my feet into. The food in Montreal; the food is something I always have to get into. The bagels are sensational. Often, I go from the airport to the bagel factory. There's a fantastic feeling in downtown Montreal, especially in the French quarter, because of all the cultures that are going on. There's a great energy and I always have to soak some of that up. And I can't wait to get back into a canoe on Brome Lake. They are all simple things, but old, old associations that are almost rituals I have to perform every time I go back.'

And the most nourishing ritual for Wendy was just a few hours away.

Wendy's excitement grew as the city petered out along the highway. Crossing the Jacques Cartier Bridge, the beginnings of the country landscape reminded her she had been travelling this road all her life.

'It gets lusher and greener and you start seeing the French Quebec farmhouses which have a very distinct look, like the buildings of New Hampshire; big wooden houses all painted sky blue and deep burgundy. And lots of big barns. The sky is clear and it's such a familiar road and it smells different. I start jumping out of my skin.'

When Wendy arrived at her mother's home, though she noted the garden was a little different and the weatherboard house had been painted anew, she felt the familiar cracks in the driveway under her feet, the rush of the mountain air in her lungs, and she clapped her eyes on that big, welcoming door, all that now stood between her and her mother. She took a leaping step up onto the stoop and knocked, then bent over double in excitement, letting out that laugh of joy again. And as Joan opened the door and reached for her daughter, she laughed. It was the loud, infectious laughter that always accompanied Wendy and Joan Matthews' reunions, the sound of their voices melding like a choir.

They held each other until the laughter turned into

tears. 'Oh, don't you start!' said Wendy, before her mother held her away and studied her.

'Let me look at you. Have you put on weight?'

Wendy, giggling, did the embarrassed daughter thing. 'Oh, don't be a mother now!'

'Well, that's what I am!' said Joan and they dissolved into giggles again and melted into a hug. They moved out into the garden, and stayed there, relishing a wonderful, soul-warming catch up, until the sun went down on the perfect Canadian day.

Practising being in the now, Joan Matthews embraces her daughter

At sixty-nine years of age, Joan Matthews was a striking, naturally beautiful woman, with a mass of silver-white curls falling to her shoulders. After her marriage ended, Joan had embarked upon her own journey. Wendy had left home, and having seen to the needs of the boys, Joan had found herself physically run down, so she began to look into holistic healing. The investigation had led her to the foothills of the Himalayas in India where she received her yoga instruction. After a stint receiving further instruction in San Francisco, she returned to Montreal. She now lived in the home in which she grew up as a child; the house that had belonged to Wendy's grandfather George, who passed away in 1985. With glorious stretches of lawn easing down a hill into town, picture-book trees and a house imbued with years of laughter and love, this was one of Wendy's favourite places in the world. And Joan's, too. That's why she'd moved in there and built a yoga school on the property where she instructed the locals.

Joan was a spiritual seeker and had lately been finding great inspiration in Eckhart Tolle's book, *The Power of Now*.

'This is so amusing because I am absolutely captivated with this book,' she said. 'It really complements the work I do and my belief system. It's all about being in the now and he gives you techniques to do that.' Joan broke into a huge smile. 'So I'd be practising being in the now and then I'd say, "Oh my God, Wendy's coming!" So there's been a huge level of anticipation and excitement. I love it when she comes. I just love it. I've been very excited . . .

But practising being in the now,' she laughed at the irony.

Wendy felt her whole being relax in the now, as she sat there chatting with her mother. 'The first two days at my mother's place is always about sleeping and sitting in the garden and long walks. She's not a very mumsy mum. Every decade or so she'll break down and it's, "I never bake cakes. I never do the ironing." She has this thing that she wasn't a good mother because she didn't bake or darn,' Wendy said laughing. 'But of course, she has been amazing. And now she's vegetarian and she loves to fortify me. And I must say it's my saving grace for my first week back.'

In return, Joan took fortification from the luxury of having her daughter right next to her and all to herself. And then the pleasure of admiring her continuing development as a lovely human being.

'Each time I see her again, it's Wendy and it's my daughter but it's almost like a new person with a whole history and bank of experience that we can explore,' said Joan. 'When we talk on the phone I hear a woman that I don't see very much and a person I miss. But we have missed out on all those years where people go through a lot together and they almost get really used to each other; there's nothing fresh and vibrant and new. And this way, it's always exciting and vibrant and new and we have lots of things to share with each other. So in those ways the distance has strengthened our relationship.'

Seeing her mother, Wendy was always reminded of how, ever since she was little, people had said they looked alike. She noted, too, with great admiration, the strength and depth of her mother's personality. There was a magnetism to Joan Matthews that made her very popular in her small community and beyond. Wendy's friends loved meeting her mother. She was not matriarchal at all; more a friend. In the way that Joan had let Wendy go busking when she was fifteen, and perhaps in the way Joan was not a 'mumsy mum', she had never been one for any rank-pulling based purely on seniority. There were no false authority structures in Joan Matthews' life. As a yoga devotee, she consciously sought to operate from a base of love and compassion, and though she was only human and sometimes faltered, her intentions shone through in her actions. With recognition of her own individuality had come respect for the individuality of others. She was a positively powerful woman.

As an adult, Wendy loved that in her mother. As a child, she had sometimes found the admiration she felt for her mother overwhelming.

'Throughout my childhood I revered her so much, I couldn't figure out where I stopped and where she began, and most of the things I did to be a good person were because my mother told me I should. So I really had to break away from that. We were so close when I was a young teen that, in retrospect, it was really necessary for me to go. I realise that now and so does she, and it's enabled us to come together whenever afterwards.'

Indeed, it was in that coming together, in coming home that she realised these things about herself. She could reassess who she was and what her responses were and why. Walking down the charming main street of Sutton, where time might have stopped, except for the houses that had crept up the hill towards her mother's once isolated home, Wendy could feel like Alice in Wonderland, grown bigger, an awkward fit, in the place she once belonged.

'Visiting my old life, I am forced to be a little bit more objective about who the hell has come home this time. Although of course things change at home, there are constants and they give me a measure of where I've been, against where I've come from. It's one of the few situations where I can be objective and actually see myself.'

And what she saw on these adult trips, this one in particular, was the complete circle: a woman who had given herself space to be herself so she could finally be comfortable being like her mother.

'We are so similar,' smiled Wendy. 'And we can talk about anything. She really is the one person in the world who can just set me straight on most things. And even if she doesn't set me straight, you know how different people bring out different aspects of you? She somehow knows how to bring out my higher self and I think that's a real gift. To have one's mother be that person has been a real strong thing for me.

'But when I go back now, I see that she's also just a human being. I think with what I've forged with my life, we are able to look at what each of us has done and respect that. I feel a little bit more of an adult with my mother now and sometimes I can actually look after her or calm her down, which has been a real revelation to me – that sometimes, I guess, I know best.'

And sometimes, they could still lock horns, because, after all, they were two strong individuals, two strong women.

'I'd love to build her a little house with a garden on my property. I'd love to have her influence in my life in Australia,' said Wendy. Joan had flirted with the idea, too, exploring the notion as a distinct possibility. 'Although,' said Wendy, 'in our moments we're so similar that we also drive each other a bit nuts, which we're very open about, thank God. We can be now. And we talk about it through distance, through our emails. With the safety of distance you can plan and dream away, but when she comes out to Australia and we spend weeks and weeks together there's some hotspots.'

Wendy could laugh about these hotspots, though, because she felt in her heart the essence of a vibrant, living relationship that would, of course, involve ups and downs. 'I've worked very hard through my life to try and separate the two of us and love her for who she is and try and figure out who the hell I am. But when I get back together with my family, everybody kind of jumps into their old dynamics and all of a sudden we're ten again. And yet I've lived more of my life away from them than with them and I've completely changed the things that colour the way they expect me to act or respond and I'm very aware of having changed. So when I get together, my mother – and I do it, too, some-times – unconsciously, we'll try and put each other back into the old box. And I'm not going there. I've worked hard to get out of it. That sort of stuff raises its head, though, and actually, last time we were together we looked at each other and she said, "You know, I don't know if I'd want to come and live with you." And I said, "I don't know if I want you to come and live with me".' Wendy collapsed into her easy laugh at the memory because, in truth, both women were easy with their similarities, easy with their differences, easy with each other. Of course, they were going to annoy each other sometimes. And they were easy with that, too.

Wendy believed that the simple things in life were often the best, like cuddling Gary's kids, her two nephews. There was Sam, the youngest, the one with the penchant for dressing up like a bee or a superhero or whatever took his fancy, as long as it involved face paint and capes, and who liked to communicate mostly through a succession of duck noises. When painfully shy, be a duck! And the other, Evan, was at the beginning of the girl-germ phase, and scrunched up his face, pulling away dramatically every time Wendy tried to kiss him. He didn't pull too hard, however, stopping just short of emancipation so he could, in fact, receive a smooch from his aunty.

They were small moments but family moments, and for the family member living at a distance, they were moments to be cherished.

For Wendy, an early breakfast of pancakes and maple syrup and bacon and eggs around a kitchen table shared with Gary and the family before they went off to school and work, was better than a six-course extravaganza served in a fancy restaurant. Standing by the kitchen sink with her mother, waiting for the kettle to boil, preparing food, bursting forth for the fun of it with a rousing rendition of 'Take Me Off To The Ball Game' while making tea was special. Just sitting down to a family dinner could become a source of enormous joy and satisfaction for Wendy, and of self-reflection, for better or worse. Dinner-table banter often revealed another priceless thing about family, of people who had known you all their lives: the inbuilt, well-honed bullshit detector.

'The questions from my family about my life,' laughed Wendy, 'they really make me think of things in such simple terms. My family are my foundation and always have been, so when they ask simple questions about my life and the way I view things, I really have to think in simple terms, get back to basics with these people I've always been able to relate to. Listening to their questions, I see how I may have veered off into other things and ways of communicating – into bullshit basically,' she laughed again. 'Talking with them just brings me back to this absolute simplicity where I am forced to think, oh well, ah, that's a good question. They make me look at my work and my motives for doing things. They'll pull me up on something that is a presumption or a given in the music industry as a way of doing things that God knows, I don't even think about any more. And you're really made to look at it and made to explain to somebody, the basis of things you take for granted. And sometimes it sounds absurd and you think, okay, I've got to rework that one. That's not right at all.'

Likewise, being able to sit under the trees and walk in the fields of her childhood was a simple pleasure that held great resonance for Wendy. The landscape she looked out on here was the same landscape in which the Native Canadians before her had walked, hunted, fished. Being in this place afforded her the opportunity to touch this aspect of herself. It had done since she was a child.

'My mother's side of the family is directly Scottish and Spanish,' said Wendy, as she sat in the long, breeze-swept grass under ancient trees, not far from her mother's house. 'And a part of my father's side is Cajun, which is kind of French mountain people really. And a while back, there was a family member who fell in love with and married an Abanaki Indian, but at the time it was very hush-hush interracial stuff. So it's a pretty small, but to me, very, very significant thread.

'As a kid, before I knew I had Abanaki blood, I would be in tears on my knees whenever the Indians got shot in the cowboy and Indian movies. And I'd always wear my hair in plaits and want my mother to take us to reservations,' she laughed. 'I loved the feeling of sitting in tepees and never really understood why it felt so strong and deep.

'My mother and I did a little bit of a pilgrimage up to the Appalachian mountains a few years back, the area the Abanakis originally came from. And it just somehow put something to rest for me. It explained why I've got

'It fills me right up to think of living among all this'

shelves and shelves of books on different tribes and where they came from, where they lived et cetera.

'But my mother and I discovered it only a few years back. And I come up to this place and just listen to the wind and the babbling brooks and look at the mists. It just fills me right up to think of living among all this, and adapting and eating with the changing seasons. I tend to live in other times in my fantasies a lot, so it thrills me to the bone to come to such an evocative place. It's a special spot.'

Wendy's grandfather had always been someone who set her straight. Her mother's father, George, a man with an avid interest in the world around him, a curious mind and an artist's eye for photography, provided many of the bedrocks of Wendy's being. Going to that house in Sutton that used to be his meant being closer to the essence of him and in turn she felt closer to the essence of herself. Every time she visited, she went through the trunk that contained a small collection of treasures from his life: prized books, sheet music, photos he had taken of his grandchildren, his camera; remnants of a life well lived, the tangible clues of that essence.

'He gave me my interest in nature. He used to say there was nothing that could not be solved or learned from nature, but we had just grown too far away from it to see that,' smiled Wendy. 'And he also gave me my interest in music. He taught me a lot of old Scottish folk songs.'

Later that day, with her brother Gary she visited the grassy Sutton cemetery where her grandfather was buried in a tree-shaded row. 'I wrote a letter to him from Los Angeles telling him how much he meant to me,' Wendy said. 'And I was so glad I did that because within a week of him receiving it, he died.'

But Wendy did not regret her absence when he passed

away. Nor would George have wanted her to, because he was a student of life and had encouraged Wendy to be one, too. He had been absolute in his belief that one should make the most out of life and if that meant going to Australia, or going to India as Joan did, well, then so be it. He believed that regrets came in what you didn't do rather than in what you did.

Visiting her grandfather's grave, while tinged with sadness, was not about missing or yearning, though those things played their part. The overall experience was more about celebrating and honouring. And just dropping in to say hi. Pretty much the things going home was about for Wendy. The only problem was, after dropping in and saying hi, she'd then have to say goodbye.

Wendy would always say goodbye in Canada. Of that, she was certain. She was an Australian citizen now and, though she'd retained her Canadian citizenship, she knew which way was home for her. 'There was a whole group of us approached about taking citizenship: there was Rachel Ward and Mark Lizotte and Greta Scaachi and myself. They changed the law. You no longer had to relinquish your original citizenship, which I wasn't prepared to do. They changed the law also so you don't have to pledge allegiance to the Queen. And basically a lot of people were afraid to come forward and do it because they felt it was a trick or something. But anyway, we all said yes as long as we could keep dual citizenship.

'I did it because Australia is where I live. Australia is where the bulk of my work is. It is my home.'

The more Wendy went back to Canada, the more she knew that would not change. 'I can't really relate to the general feeling of the people here any more. I can only barely remember the feeling of the times when I could,' she told Eden. She was sitting in the living room, the camera rolling, her mother off in the kitchen. 'There are very, very different ways and different sensibilities here, and I can relate much more to the Australian way, strangely enough, a lot more than I can the Canadian way. I remember things, similarities, and I remember that I once felt part of it. I love that this is where my family is. But I can't really relate to the country's general personality.'

Later, Wendy admitted that this statement was perhaps the first time she had articulated her feelings on the matter, and she'd found it difficult.

'That was really hard for me to say on camera. I didn't know I was going to say it. And I felt really conscious of my mother being in the kitchen hearing me say, "No, I couldn't come back here to live." I'd been talking about how much these people meant to me and how we were scattered all over the world and how with getting older, with the passing of time, you realised that there was less sense in not being together. So I had a really hard time saying that, but it was a revelation for me. I realised that I've got this romantic notion of where I've come from in my childhood and my formative years are so precious to me. I've got such incredible memories, and Canada and that area and my family are very special to me and I get so much out of going back. And sometimes in my life, you know, all I want to do is go and curl up in my mother's wedding dress or something. And there I was, saying I couldn't go back there to live.

'But I realised that Australia is my home. It is that simple.' She smiled with an afterthought. 'And that complex.'

'She can never stay long enough,' said Joan Matthews. 'The longest we had was three weeks and that was some time ago. When the boys come home, even though they're the ages they are, they're playful and they jump off furniture and wrestle each other and grab each other and when Wendy's here, she's a part of that. To see them, my heart gets so full, but within that, I'm already thinking, oh my god, they're going to have to leave. And when I see Wendy leave for the airport it's like when she left when she was fifteen and a half. My heart is wrenched and it does get harder. As I get older, it gets harder because when you're in your seventieth year you can say, well, maybe another ten years.'

Wendy was now leaving again. There on the driveway, they hugged their final hugs, squeezing as much as they could out of them, holding each other as long as possible, taking the warmth, the feeling of the other person, the moment, and imprinting it in mind, heart and soul. Both Wendy and Joan made an effort to smile, to make that last moment memorable, to make sure the last thing each got from the other was that smile.

But it was hard. It always was.

And harder still, those hours after Wendy left, when Joan sat by the fire, thinking about the visit and the wonderful times shared, and letting the tears fall. It was virtually impossible to practise being in the now. And just as difficult for Wendy was the drive back to Montreal to catch her flight, then the long hours in the air between Canada and Australia, thinking the same thoughts, shedding tears salted with the same sadness.

'I feel like I'm always saying goodbye, either here or back in Australia,' Wendy said. 'But that's part of life.'

Wendy Matthews' biggest hit was the song 'The Day You Went Away'. She didn't write that song, but her haunting, exquisite interpretation of it claimed it as hers. She understood the lyrics so well. She sang that song about missing and leaving and the moment of goodbye with the force of all the many moments in her memory that connected to it, and she sang it knowing very much that it is part of life.

Less than a year after shooting Wendy's documentary for *The Ties That Bind*, Joan Matthews turned seventy and Wendy flew home again for the grand occasion and celebration.

'Her whole community put this dinner on for her,' smiled Wendy in wonder. 'There were one hundred and thirty people and there was a waiting list! It was phenomenal. And I thought, this woman has built up this whole thing here; an extraordinary network of really very supportive and loving people. I mean, my last birthday wasn't a big year or anything, but it was like two people and a dog!' she laughed. 'But as an adult you can look at your parents in those circumstances and see them not as parents, but as people who have accomplished this much in life, who have created such wonderful connections for themselves. I felt so proud. So very proud. And it makes me feel better, her turning seventy and me being at the opposite end of the globe, just knowing how loved she is in her community. She's a celebrity!'

Wendy, of course, was a bit of a celebrity, too, being the occasional visitor. 'It's such an intense time when I go back there. We all love each other so much, it's just never enough and it's all go-go-go in a way.'

But there was another special guest at the party: Wendy's dad Peter. 'He turned up unannounced and completely out of the blue,' laughed Wendy. 'And I love him for all that. I think he's an extraordinary human being.

'We hadn't all stood in the same room for, my God, so long. My older brother and my father are both photographers, so all of a sudden we just looked at each other and Dad and Gary said at once, "Take a picture!" and we all laughed.

'I thought that was great for my dad, because taking the family photo, that's so my father. As kids we were all plagued by him documenting our childhood with his photography. And in all of them, we all looked like children of the Depression, sitting there all rolling our eyes, going, "Daaaaad". But of course, now I'm so grateful that he did.

'A few years back he put together these extraordinary albums, one for me, one for Gary, one for Glenn, and it was our childhood, things that I'd completely forgotten and had no idea that he'd documented. All of us looked incredibly grumpy, I'd like to add. I could kill us for that.

'But that didn't stop us. Even at my mother's seventieth, we all went, "Daaaaad".'

That's family. Wendy's family. And though she lives on the other side of the world, her cup is filled by them.

About the author

Julietta Jameson is one of Australia's most experienced journalists. She has crossed the gamut of Australian media, working in radio, television and the print medium. She has been a foreign correspondent based in the United States, arts editor and columnist, and has been published in many Australian magazines and metropolitan newspapers. She is the author of two previously published books: a non-fiction work titled *Tibooburra and the Legend of the Tree of Knowledge*; and a novel titled *In Her Mother's House*.

Acknowledgements

Thank you, Eden Gaha, for your incredible generosity and faith in handing over your baby.

And thanks to all the other wonderful people who opened up for this book – you inspired me far beyond your chapters:

Jay, Pofitu, and the whole Laga'aia clan for the big family love and excellent barbecue;

Wendy Matthews for awesome honesty and courage. To the rest of the Matthews family for giving us Wendy!

Mary Coustas for your eloquent candidness; Theophani Coustas for letting me into your 'very popular' life;

Cindy and Ching-Lee Pan, who made me laugh so hard despite my flu. Thanks for the many cups of tea with honey;

Craig Wing – go you good thing! Editha and Allan Wing for bringing up a fine young man, and for being the fine human beings you are.

Special thanks to David Kelly for all the pearls;

Fiona Henderson at Bantam Doubleday whose passion for this project knew no bounds, editor Kim Swivel, project editor Sophie Ambrose, and Tina Jantke for the lovely page design.

A big prayer of gratitude for the departed loved ones: Naseeb Gaha, Steve Coustas and Finuaga Laga'aia, whose proud spirits pervade these pages; and to the traditional owners of Australia whose spirit is the bedrock of this book.

Thank you Nicola Gaha and Dawn Herman.

Special thanks to my agent, Selwa Anthony, whose instincts and kindness continue to astonish me.

Thank you Gram Parsons.

And thank you, always and ever, the magnificent universal energy that provided all of the above.